Weighed In Productions in associati
the Finborough Theatre presents

The first UK production in 75 years

THE WIND OF HEAVEN

by
Emlyn Williams

FINBOROUGH | THEATRE
VIBRANT **NEW WRITING** | UNIQUE **REDISCOVERIES**

First performance at the St James's Theatre: Thursday, 12 April 1945.
First performance at the Finborough Theatre: Tuesday, 26 November 2019.

Please turn your mobile phones off - the light they emit can also be distracting.

Our patrons are respectfully reminded that, in this intimate theatre, any noise such as the rustling of programmes, food packaging or talking may distract the actors and your fellow audience members.

We regret there is no admittance or re-admittance to the auditorium whilst the performance is in progress.

The Wind of Heaven

by
Emlyn Williams

Cast in order of speaking

Menna	**Kristy Philipps**
Dilys	**Rhiannon Neads**
Bet	**Louise Breckon-Richards**
Pitter	**David Whitworth**
Ambrose	**Jamie Wilkes**
Evan	**Seiriol Tomos**
Mrs Lake	**Melissa Woodbridge**
Gwyn	**Benedict Barker**
Gwyn	**Bruno Ben Tovim**

The action takes place in the Welsh mountain village of Blestin, in the summer of 1856, soon after the end of the Crimean War.

Scene 1. Morning.
Scene 2. Evening of the same day.
Scene 3. Early the next morning.

Scene 4. Some hours afterwards; early evening.
Scene 5. Two days later; deep in the night.
Scene 6. Early the following evening.

There will be one interval of fifteen minutes.

Director	**Will Maynard**
Designer	**Ceci Calf**
Costume Designer	**Isobel Pellow**
Lighting Designer	**Ryan Joseph Stafford**
Composer and Sound Designer	**Julian Starr**
Composer and Musical Director	**Rhiannon Drake**
Co-Producer	**Bertie Taylor-Smith**
Co-Producer	**Jonathan Taylor**
Executive Producer	**Tom Bevan**
Stage Manager	**Charlotte Brown**
Assistant Stage Manager	**Chloe Seyer**
Assistant Director and	**Myles O'Gorman**
Deputy Stage Manager	

Please see front of house notices or ask an usher for an exact running time.

Louise Breckon-Richards | Bet

Trained at Guildhall School of Music and Drama.
Theatre includes *Can You Hear Me Running?*
(Pleasance London), *Haunted Hotel* (Mercury Theatre,
Colchester), *The Merchant of Venice* (Kiklos Teatro,
Italy), *Romeo and Juliet* (English Shakespeare
Company), *A Little Night Music, Under Milk Wood,
Happy Birthday Brecht* (National Theatre), *The Sound
of Music* (West Yorkshire Playhouse), *Northanger
Abbey* (Queen's Theatre, Hornchurch) and *The Boys
from Syracuse* (Harrogate Theatre).
Film includes *Time Will Tell, To Kill a King* and *Beautiful
People.*
Television includes *Doctors, Coronation Street, Temple,
Cuckoo, EastEnders, Sherlock, Casualty, Midsomer
Murders, Dirty War, Foyle's War, Battlefield Britain,
Family Affairs, Bed Time, Belonging, Holby City,
Mortimer's Law, Underworld* and *Harpur and Iles.*
Radio includes *Precious Bane* and *The Room with a
View.*
Writing includes *Four O'Clock Flowers* (Space Arts
Centre), *Trace* (Old Diorama Theatre), *The Cloak of
Visibility* (Mountview Catalyst Festival) and a new
commission for Mountview Academy of Theatre Arts
for 2020.

Rhiannon Neads | Dilys

Trained at LAMDA.
Theatre includes *3 Billion Seconds* (Paines Plough
Roundabout), *Leia and the Roman* (Vaults Festival),
Adele is Younger than Us (Soho Theatre), *Mary's
Babies* (Oak Theatre), *By All Accounts Two Normal
Girls* (Stiff and Kitsch at Edinburgh Festival), *Madonna
and Child* (Monday Club) and *1001* (Courting Drama at
Southwark Playhouse).
Television includes *Father Brown, Doctors, Midsomer
Murders* and *Downton Abbey.*
Radio includes *Home Front, A Severed Head, The
Stuarts – Queen Anne: Myself Alone, Baby Oil, The
Last Chronicle of Barset, The Enchanted April, A Book
by Lester Tricklebank, Born in the DDR, The Master
and Margarita, Decline and Fall, In Aldershot* and
Ladder of Years.

Kristy Philipps | Menna

Trained at the Royal Welsh College of Music and Drama.
Theatre includes *The Devil in the Blue Dress* (Bunker
Theatre).
Television includes *Will, Cleaning Up, Informer* and
Vera.

Seiriol Tomos | Evan
Productions at the Finborough Theatre include *Saer Doliau*.
Trained at LAMDA.
Theatre includes *Tuck* (Neontopia), *Milwr Yn Y Meddwl*, *The Lady From the Sea* and *The Tempest* (National Theatre Wales).
Film includes *The Dancing Floor*, *Merthyr*, *X-Row*, *Woman of the Wolf* and *Elenya*.
Television includes *Mofydd*, *Parch II*, *Hinterland*, *Gwaith or Cartref*, *Rownd A Rownd*, *Pobol Y Cwm* and *Britain's Secret Houses*.

David Whitworth | Pitter
Productions at the Finborough Theatre include *London Wall* (and its subsequent transfer to the St James Theatre, now known as The Other Palace) and *Rigor Mortis*.
Theatre includes *Skin in the Game* (Old Red Lion Theatre), *The Second Mrs Tanqueray* (Rose Theatre, Kingston), *London Assurance* (National Theatre), *Wuthering Heights* (Birmingham Rep and National Tour), *The Mousetrap* (St Martin's Theatre), *Pride and Prejudice*, *Romeo and Juliet*, *Twelfth Night*, *Much Ado About Nothing*, *A Midsummer Night's Dream*, *Henry V*, *As You Like It*, *The Dark Lady of the Sonnets*, *Love's Labours Lost*, *The Two Noble Kinsmen* (Open Air Theatre, Regent's Park), *Lilies and Sweets* (Pleasance London), *A Day by the Sea* (Southwark Playhouse), *French Without Tears* (English Touring Theatre), *Read Not Dead* (Shakespeare's Globe), *In the Bar of a Tokyo Hotel* (Charing Cross Theatre), *Aladdin*, *Sleeping Beauty* (National Tour), *The Woman in Black* (Gothenburg English Studio Theatre and Stadsteater, Stockholm), *French Without Tears*, *The Widowing of Mrs Holroyd*, *The Thunderbolt*, *Mary Goes First*, *A Journey to London*, *Double Double*, *Trifles*, *Sauce for the Goose*, *King Lear* and *Magnificence* (Orange Tree Theatre, Richmond).
Film includes *Love's Kitchen* and *Little Dorrit*.
Television includes *The Alan Titchmarsh Show*, *Poldark*, *The Bill*, *Nicholas Nickleby*, *Jasper Carrott*, *Big Deal*, *Miss Jones and Son*, *Colditz*, *Z Cars*, *Coronation Street*, *A Family at War*, *Barlow* and *Armchair Theatre*.

Jamie Wilkes | Ambrose
Trained at LAMDA.
Theatre includes *The Edit* (Salisbury Playhouse),
*The Two Noble Kinsmen, The Rover, Oppenheimer,
The Shoemaker's Holiday, Wendy and Peter Pan*
(Royal Shakespeare Company), *The Comedy of
Errors, Titus Andronicus* (Shakespeare's Globe),
*Diary of a Teenage Girl, Howl's Moving Castle,
The Boy James, Lorca is Dead, Atrium, Tartuffe*
(Southwark Playhouse), *Peter Pan, The Beggar's
Opera, Macbeth* (Theatre Royal York), *Dracula*
(Edinburgh International Festival), *Metamorphosis*
(National Student Drama Festival Spotlight Award for
Best Actor), *Romeo and Juliet, As You Like It, The
Tempest, Julius Caesar, The Taming of the Shrew,
Love's Labour's Lost* (Willow Globe), *Macbeth,
A Midsummer Night's Dream, The Tempest,
Antigone, Bensalem B&B, The Trial and The Tempest*
(Belt Up Theatre).
Television includes *His Dark Materials, Catch 22,
Vanity Fair, Philip K Dick's Electric Dreams,
Mr Selfridge* and *Downton Abbey*.
Radio includes *Homefront*.

Melissa Woodbridge | Mrs Lake
Trained at Royal Scottish Academy of Music and
Drama.
Theatre includes *Walking the Tightrope, Blithe
Spirit* (US Tour), *Giraffe* (Park Theatre), *Blithe Spirit*
(Gielgud Theatre), *Ironman* (Pleasance Theatre),
Strands (Theatre503), *Skanky* (Arcola Theatre),
Kvetch (King's Head Theatre), *A Cello* (The Yard),
The Female of the Species (Vaudeville Theatre),
Leonardo's Canyon (Royal Court Theatre), *Straight
Talking* and *Moving the Goalposts* (Soho Theatre).
Film includes *The Angel, Another Table* and *Someone
To Watch Over Me*.
Television includes *Be in the Now, Touching the Cloth*
and *This is Not a List Show*.

Benedict Barker | Gwyn
Benedict is currently training at Sylvia Young Theatre School.

Bruno Ben Tovim | Gwyn
Bruno is currently training at Sylvia Young Theatre School.

Emlyn Williams | Playwright

Productions at the Finborough Theatre include *Accolade* and *The Druid's Rest*.

From the time of his definitive success in 1935 in his own play *Night Must Fall*, Emlyn Williams was an out-standing figure in the British and American theatre as actor, playwright and director. His other plays include *The Light of Heart*, *Spring 1600*, *Someone Waiting* and *The Corn Is Green*, in which he starred with Sybil Thorndike in London.

The American production starred Ethel Barrymore and the play was filmed with Bette Davis and – later – Katharine Hepburn.

Numerous stage appearances in London and New York included The *Winslow Boy* by Terence Rattigan and *Montserrat* by Lillian Hellman, while his films include *The Citadel*, *The Stars Look Down*, *Major Barbara*, *Hatter's Castle*, *Ivanhoe*, *The Last Days of Dolwyn* (which he also directed, having written it for Edith Evans and Richard Burton), and an historical curiosity, the unfinished *I Claudius*.

In 1951 he embarked on a solo performance as *Charles Dickens Enacting Scenes from his Stories*, a pioneering venture so successful that it took him all over the world, as did his second similar venture as *Dylan Thomas Growing Up*.

In between these tours he appeared in a Shakespeare season at Stratford-upon-Avon, in *A Man For All Seasons* and *The Deputy* in New York, and in London in his own adaptation of Turgenev's *A Month In The Country* with Ingrid Bergman and Michael Redgrave. His adaptation of *The Master Builder* was presented by the National Theatre with Laurence Olivier, Maggie Smith, Joan Plowright and Michael Redgrave.

Later film appearances included *The Deep Blue Sea* (with Vivien Leigh), *I Accuse* (with Jose Ferrer), *The Wreck Of The Mary Deare* (with Gary Cooper), *The L-Shaped Room* (with Leslie Caron) and *The Eye Of The Devil* (with Deborah Kerr).

In 1961, he was a commentator at the televised Investiture of the Prince of Wales. Later television appear-ances included *The Deadly Game* and *Rumpole of The Bailey*.

He also wrote two volumes of autobiography, *George and Emlyn*, a novel, *Headlong and Beyond Belief (A Chronicle of Murder and its Detection)*.

Emlyn Williams was made CBE in 1962 and died in 1987.

For many years, he lived at Flat 3, 123 Dovehouse Street, Chelsea, London, about ten minutes walk from the Finborough Theatre.

Will Maynard | Director

Trained at Oxford School of Drama.

Direction includes *Open* (Vaults Festival), *Head-Rot Holiday* (Hope Theatre), *Tiger* (Vaults Festival), *Finding Mr Hart* (Blackburn Exchange for the University of London), *Blavatsky's Tower* (Barons Court Theatre), *Classical Studies* (Arcola Theatre), *Crocodile* (Old

Red Lion Theatre), *Sunflower* (Bunker Theatre) and *Gold Star* (Hen and Chickens Theatre).
Assistant Direction includes *Bloody Poetry* (Jermyn Street Theatre) and *Mary Rose* (Brockley Jack Theatre).

Ceci Calf | Designer
Trained at the Royal Welsh College of Music and Drama.
Designs include *Five Green Bottles*, *Tithonus* (Sherman Theatre, Cardiff), *Cheer, Mydidae* (The Other Room, Cardiff), *The Cut* (LAMDA and the Lion and Unicorn Theatre) and *Yellow Moon* (LAMDA).
Forthcoming productions include *One Million Tiny Plays About Britain* (Jermyn Street Theatre and the Watermill Theatre, Newbury).

Isobel Pellow | Costume Designer
Trained at London College of Fashion.
Theatre Costume Design includes *Lysistrata* (Cockpit Theatre), *Heather and Harry* (Camden People's Theatre), *King Lear* (Pleasure Dome Theatre Company), *'Tis Pity She's A Whore* (Tristan Bates Theatre), *Three Brothers* (Theatre N16), *The Xmas Carol* (Old Red Lion Theatre), *Sense and Sensibility, Mary Stuart* and *A Streetcar Named Desire* (Oxford Playhouse), *Blue Stockings, Hay Fever* (Old Fire Station Theatre, Oxford) and *The Accrington Pals* (Ashcroft Theatre, Croydon). Opera Costume Design includes *Tales of Offenbach* (Opera Della Luna at Wilton's Music Hall).
Film Costume Design includes *Deos Novos* (Audiomotion) and *The Wait for Midnight Thirteen* (DeCantillon Films).
Theatre Costume Supervision includes *The Sweet Science of Bruising* (Wilton's Music Hall), *Five Plays* (The Young Vic), *Britten in Brooklyn* (Wilton's Music Hall), *Four Play* and *Clickbait* (Theatre503). Opera Costume Supervision includes *The Crowning of Poppea* (Hampstead Garden Opera at Jackson's Lane Theatre).
Costume Assistant work includes *East Wall* (Hofesh Shechter Company at the Tower of London), *Ottone and Life on the Moon* (English Touring Opera) and *The Little Witch* (The Place).

Ryan Joseph Stafford | Lighting Designer
Trained at Rose Bruford College.
Recent designs include *CODI* (National Dance Company Wales), *Cyrano de Bergerac* (Watermill Theatre, Newbury), *Together, Not the Same* (Sadler's Wells Theatre), *Left from Write* (Norwegian National Ballet II and Linbury Studio Theatre, Royal Opera House), *Crave* (The Other Room and the Royal Welsh College of Music

and Drama), *Hauntings and Pork Pies* (Theatr Clwyd and National Trust), *Becoming* (Stratford Circus), *Pippin* (University of Wales Trinity Saint David, Cardiff), *Robin Hood, Easy Virtue* (Watermill Theatre, Newbury), *The Island* (Fio and National Tour), *Cardiff Boy* (Red Oak Theatre and The Other Room), *The Secret Lives of Baba Segi's Wives* (Elufowoju, Jr. Ensemble at Arcola Theatre), *Dames* (Siberian Lights at Pleasance London), *Finding Mr Hart* (Blackburn Cotton Exchange), *The River* (Red Oak Theatre) and *Landmines* (Ovalhouse).

Julian Starr | Composer and Sound Designer
Previous productions at the Finborough Theatre include *A Winning Hazard* and *After Dark*.
Trained at the Australian National Institute of Dramatic Arts.
Theatre includes *ZOG* (National Tour), *Othello* (Union Theatre), *Cry Havoc, Hell Yes I'm Tough Enough* (Park Theatre), *Violet* (National Tour), *Aisha* for which he received an OffWestEnd Award Nomination for Best Sound Design (London Tour), *The Orchestra* (Omnibus Theatre), *Alice In Slasherland* (Old Fitz Theatre, Sydney), *White Noise* (Vaults Festival), *The Boy Under The Christmas Tree* (Kings Head Theatre), *Tiger Under My Skin* (Bloomsbury Theatre), *The Giant Killers* (National Tour), *Eris* (Bunker Theatre), *Gulliver Returns* (National Tour), *You Only Live Forever* (National Tour and Soho Theatre), *Surf Seance* (Sydney Arts Festival), *The Comedy of Errors*, *Pericles* (National Tour and Czech Republic Tour), *Precious Little* (Brockley Jack Theatre), *The Good Scout* (Above the Stag and Edinburgh Fringe Festival), *The Shifting Heart* (Seymour Centre Sydney), *Untold* (Playhouse Theatre Sydney), *Kapow* (Kings Cross Theatre, Sydney), *Telescope* (Old Fitz Theatre, Sydney), *Best Before* (Sydney Fringe Festival) and *The Shadow Box* (Old Fitz Theatre, Sydney).
Design Assistant and Associate include *Mama Mia! The Musical* (Capital Theatre Sydney), *Disney's Aladdin The Musical* (Queensland QPAC), *Talk*, *Richard III* (Sydney Opera House), *The Royal Edinburgh Military Tattoo* (Edinburgh Castle) and *An Inspector Calls* (UK and Ireland Tour).

Rhiannon Drake | Composer and Musical Director
Trained at the Arts Educational Schools, London, following a Geography degree at the University of Oxford.
Compositions include *The Year Without A Summer* (Above The Arts Theatre, and original cast recording), *Herstoric* (Drayton Arms Theatre) *Gwen* (The Ceiling Project, Bishopsgate Institute).
Composition as collaborator include *And You Were Wonderful... On Stage* (International Tour and Tate Britain).
Rhiannon also arranges music for various vocal and a cappella groups including *Viva La Vamp*, award-winners at this year's Open Mic:UK Final at the O2, who she also performs with.
Rhiannon has been composing for ten years, alongside her career as an actor-musician.
www.rhiannondrake.co.uk

Charlotte Brown | Stage Manager
Stage Management includes *Shit-Faced Showtime: Alice Through the Cocktail Glass* (Edinburgh Festival), *Endless Second* (Edinburgh Festival, Park Theatre and Pleasance London) and *I Run* (Edinburgh Festival).
Other theatre includes *Open and I Run* (Vaults Festival).
Lighting Design and Operation include *Laundry*, *South Afreakins* and *The Conductor* (The Space).
Charlotte is currently Assistant Festival Coordinator for New Nordics Festival at The Yard.

Chloe Seyer | Assistant Stage Manager
Trained at the Savannah College of Art and Design in Georgia, USA.
Theatre includes *Measure for Measure, Romeo and Juliet, Much Ado About Nothing, An Octoroon, The Eumenides* and *Top Girls*.
She co-founded Enter Messenger Theatre Company in Atlanta.

Myles O'Gorman | Assistant Director and Deputy Stage Manager
Productions at the Finborough Theatre include Production Assistant for Chemistry.
Theatre as Director includes *WoLab Actor/Writer Showcase* (Bunker Theatre), *Medea Speaks* and *Crave* (TheSpaceUK at the Edinburgh Festival), *The Winter's Tale* (The Warren, Brighton Fringe and OSO Arts Centre, Barnes), *His Dark Materials* (Fitzwilliam Museum, Cambridge), *The Oresteia* and *The Merchant of Venice* (ADC Theatre, Cambridge).

Paul Griffiths | Historical Consultation / Ymgynghoriad Hanesyddol
Paul is a Welsh writer, director and theatre critic.
Theatre includes *Masque of the Red Death* (Punchdrunk and BAC), *Frankenstein, Missing Mel* (Cochrane Theatre), *Korczak* (Rose Theatre, Kingston), *Terry Pratchett's Mort, A Winter's Tale* (Yvonne Arnaud Theatre, Guildford), *Loserville, Peter Pan, A Beggar's Opera* (South Hill Park Arts Centre) and *The Dummy Tree* (Tristan Bates Theatre).
Writing includes three musicals for Gŵyl Fai Pwllheli with Annette Bryn Parri, and two for Eisteddfod yr Urdd with Gareth Glyn and Einion Dafydd.
Film as Production Assistant includes *Brâd, Sgwâr y Sgorpion* and *Y Bitsh*
Television as Writer includes *Tipyn o Stâd, Pengelli, Bibi Bêl, B'echdan Wŷ?* and *Traeth Coch*.
Television as Director includes *Hidden Love, Eisteddfod Genedlaethol yr Urdd* and *Gŵyl Gerdd Dant*.
Television as Production Assistant includes *Jones, Jones, Jones* which received a BAFTA, *Y Sioe Gelf, Popeth yn Gymraeg, Cymru*

a'r America Gaeth, Lleifior II, Y Bitsh, Tydi Coleg yn Grêt, Tipyn o Stâd, Bob a'i Fam, Naw Tan Naw, Noson Lawen, Y*ma Mae Nghân Dafydd Iwan*: *Corsica, Diolch o Galon, Diwnod Gyda...,* Randolph Turpin, Richard Hughes, Frongoch - *Coláiste na Réabhlóide* and *Celtic Monsters.*
Radio as Writer and Director includes *Becca Bingo* and *Dan y Don.*
Paul has written numerous award-winning short plays.
Paul also spent a year working at Soho Theatre.
Paul is currently working on a full-length stage play *Annwyl Morris, Annwyl Prosser* with support from Theatr Genedlaethol Cymru.
Paul was the main theatre critic for the National Paper of Wales / *Y Cymro* for twenty years.
Paul has worked for numerous TV and Radio broadcasters including S4C, BBC Radio Cymru, ITV Wales, BBC Wales and TG4.
Between 2008 and 2012, Paul was the Operations Manager for Youth Music Theatre UK.
Paul won the Drama Medal at the National *Urdd Gobaith Cymru Eisteddfod* in Wales, three times in succession between 1995 and 1997.
Paul is a regular contributor on S4C and BBC Radio Cymru.

Tommo Fowler | Dramaturgical Support
Productions at the Finborough Theatre as director includes *Jam, I Wish To Die Singing* and *Obamaology.*
Tommo is a dramaturg for text and production, and a director. Dramaturgy includes *Out of the Dark* (Rose Theatre, Kingston), *Inside Voices* (Vaults Festival), *Griff Rhys Jones: Where Was I?* (International Tour) and *Griff Rhys Jones: Jones & Smith* (National Tour).
Tommo is currently developing new versions of *Purgatory in Ingolstadt, Pioneers in Ingolstadt* and *The Weavers,* and a new play in Hebrew, originally seen at the Finborough Theatre *Vibrant Festival, Prisoners of the Occupation.*
Tommo is a Visiting Tutor on the MA Creative Writing (Playwriting) at City University, and a script reader for the Royal Court Theatre, Bush Theatre and Bruntwood Prize.
Tommo is also co-founder of script-reading and dramaturgy company RoughHewn.
Direction includes an original adaptation of *Youth Without God* (University of Salford), *Disruption* (Kensington Karavan), *The Strip, Fear and Misery of the Third Reich* (Oxford School of Drama), *Comet* (Pleasance London) and *Mumburger* (Old Red Lion Theatre and Archivist's Gallery, Haggerston).

Andrea Hazel Lewis | Dialect Coach
Andrea trained at The Royal Central School of Speech and Drama.
Recent productions include *The Hypnotist* (London Horror Festival
at Pleasance London) and *Don Quixote in Algiers* (White Bear
Theatre).

Tom Bevan | Executive Producer
Trained at the Royal Welsh College of Music and Drama.
Theatre includes *The Internet Was Made for Adults* (Vaults Festival),
Tarot (Assembly, Edinburgh Festival), *Mojave* (Camden People's
Theatre and Reykjavik Fringe Festival), *Sugar Baby* (Soho Theatre
and Tour) and *Six: The Musical* in its original student production
(Sweet Venues, Edinburgh Festival).
Tom is currently Assistant Producer at Theatr Clwyd, Wales'
foremost producing theatre.
He is line-producing several new commissions, a tour of new
musical *Milky Peaks*, as site specific co-production with the National
Trust at Powis Castle, and artist and writer development programme
TYFU|GROW.
Tom helps to programme theatre, music, comedy and spoken word
into the venue's four performance spaces including the Emlyn
Williams Theatre.
Tom also currently leads on Social Media for ERA 50:50, a campaign
calling for gender balance on stage and screen by the end of 2020.

Bertie Taylor-Smith | Co-Producer
Trained at the Royal Welsh College of Music and Drama.
Until recently, Bertie was the Artistic Associate of Chelsea Theatre.
Productions include *Fragments Of A Complicated Mind*
(Theatre503), *Plays Without Decor: All Our Happy Days Are Stupid*
(Wilton's), *Once Upon A Snowflake*, *Camp Be Yourself* and *'Til The
Worlds End* (Chelsea Theatre).

Jonathan Taylor | Co-Producer
Jonathan is Associate Producer at Caged Bird Theatre.
Productions include *Little Shop of Horrors* (Exeter Phoenix), *NEON*
(Lion and Unicorn Theatre), *Hamlet* (Stratford Playhouse) and *The
Remarkables* (Edinburgh Festival).
Assistant Producer work includes *Exeter Fringe Festival* and *The
Claim* (James Quaife Productions).
www.taylorproductions.co.uk

Welsh Playwrights at the Finborough Theatre/ Dramodwyr Cymreig ar lwyfan Theatr Finborough

Work by Welsh playwrights at the Finborough Theatre has included *Downtown Paradise* by Mark Jenkins, subsequently seen on National Tour and at the Chapter Arts Centre, Cardiff (1996), *Y Weledigaeth* by Gavin Skerritt, performed in Welsh and the subject of a documentary for S4C (2001), the *Time Out* Critics' Choice production of *Young Emma*, an adaptation by Laura Wade of the "secret memoir" of poet W.H. Davies, specially commissioned for the Finborough Theatre (2003), two plays by former local resident Emlyn Williams – *The Druid's Rest* (2009) and *Accolade* (2011) which subsequently transferred to the St James Theatre, now The Other Palace, the English premiere of *Saer Doliau* by Gwenlyn Parry, performed in Welsh (2013), three musicals by Ivor Novello – Perchance to Dream (2011), *Gay's The Word* (2012) which was recorded and also transferred to Jermyn Street Theatre, and *Valley of Song* (2014) which also has an original cast recording available, and the world premiere of *Exodus* by Rachael Boulton (2018).

Production Acknowledgements

Dialect Coach	**Andrea Hazel Lewis**
Dramaturgical Support	**Tommo Fowler**
Historical Consultant	**Paul Griffiths**
Photography	**Stefan Hanegraff**
Copyright agent	**Alan Brodie Representation Ltd**
	www.alanbrodie.com

The company wishes to thank all the individuals and organisations who have so generously supported this production.

The Wind of Heaven © The Estate of Emlyn Williams, 1945
First presented at the St James' Theatre, London in April 1945 starring Diana Wynyard and Emlyn Williams, produced by H. M. Tennent.

FINBOROUGH | THEATRE

"Probably the most influential fringe theatre in the world."
Time Out

"Under Neil McPherson, possibly the most unsung of all major artistic directors in Britain, the Finborough has continued to plough a fertile path of new plays and rare revivals that gives it an influence disproportionate to its tiny 50-seat size."
Mark Shenton, *The Stage*

"The mighty little Finborough which, under Neil McPherson, continues to offer a mixture of neglected classics and new writing in a cannily curated mix."
Lyn Gardner, *The Stage*

"The tiny but mighty Finborough"
Ben Brantley, *The New York Times*

Photo credit: Douglas Mackie

Founded in 1980, the multi-award-winning Finborough Theatre presents plays and music theatre, concentrated exclusively on vibrant new writing and unique rediscoveries from the 19th and 20th centuries.

Our programme is unique – we never present work that has been seen anywhere in London during the last 25 years. Behind the scenes, we continue to discover and develop a new generation of theatre makers – most notably through our invitation-only Finborough Forum monthly meetings.

Despite remaining completely unsubsidised, the Finborough Theatre has an unparalleled track record for attracting the finest talent who go on to become leading voices in British theatre. Under Artistic Director Neil McPherson, it has discovered some of the UK's most exciting new playwrights including Laura Wade, James Graham, Mike Bartlett, Jack Thorne, Alexandra Wood, Nicholas de Jongh and Anders Lustgarten, and directors including Tamara Harvey, Robert Hastie, Blanche McIntyre, Kate Wasserberg and Sam Yates.

Artists working at the theatre in the 1980s included Clive Barker, Rory Bremner, Nica Burns, Kathy Burke, Ken Campbell, Jane Horrocks and Claire Dowie. In the 1990s, the Finborough Theatre first became known for new writing including Naomi Wallace's first play *The War Boys*, Rachel Weisz in David Farr's *Neville Southall's Washbag*, four plays by Anthony Neilson including *Penetrator* and *The Censor*, both of which transferred to the Royal Court Theatre, and new plays by Richard Bean, Lucinda Coxon, David Eldridge, Tony Marchant and Mark Ravenhill. New writing development included the premieres of modern classics such as Mark Ravenhill's *Shopping and F***king*, Conor McPherson's *This Lime Tree Bower*, Naomi Wallace's *Slaughter City* and Martin McDonagh's *The Pillowman*.

Since 2000, new British plays have included Laura Wade's London debut *Young Emma*, commissioned for the Finborough Theatre, two one-woman shows by Miranda Hart, James Graham's *Albert's Boy* with Victor Spinetti, Sarah Grochala's *S27*, Athena Stevens' *Schism* which was nominated for an Olivier Award, and West End transfers for Joy Wilkinson's *Fair*, Nicholas de Jongh's *Plague Over England*, Jack Thorne's *Fanny and Faggot*, Neil McPherson's Olivier Award nominated *It Is Easy To Be Dead*, and Dawn King's *Foxfinder*.

UK premieres of foreign plays have included plays by Brad Fraser, Lanford Wilson, Larry Kramer, Tennessee Williams, the English premiere of Robert McLellan's Scots language classic, *Jamie the Saxt*, and three West End transfers – Frank McGuinness' *Gates of Gold* with William Gaunt and John Bennett, and Craig Higginson's *Dream of the Dog* with Dame Janet Suzman.

Rediscoveries of neglected work – most commissioned by the Finborough Theatre – have included the first London revivals of Rolf Hochhuth's *Soldiers* and *The Representative*, both parts of Keith Dewhurst's *Lark Rise to Candleford*, *The Women's War*, an evening of original suffragette plays, *Etta Jenks* with Clarke Peters and Daniela Nardini, Noël Coward's first play *The Rat Trap*, Emlyn Williams' *Accolade*, Lennox Robinson's *Drama at Inish* with Celia Imrie and Paul O'Grady, John Van Druten's *London Wall* which transferred to St James' Theatre, and J. B. Priestley's Cornelius which transferred to a sell out Off Broadway run in New York City.

Music Theatre has included the new (premieres from Grant Olding, Charles Miller, Michael John LaChuisa, Adam Guettel, Andrew Lippa, Paul Scott Goodman, and Adam Gwon's *Ordinary Days* which transferred to the West End) and the old (the UK premiere of Rodgers and Hammerstein's *State Fair* which also transferred to the West End), and the acclaimed 'Celebrating British Music Theatre' series.

The Finborough Theatre won *The Stage* Fringe Theatre of the Year Award in 2011, *London Theatre Reviews'* Empty Space Peter Brook Award in 2010 and 2012, swept the board with eight awards at the 2012 OffWestEnd Awards, and was nominated for an Olivier Award in 2017 and 2019. Artistic Director Neil McPherson was awarded the Critics' Circle Special Award for Services to Theatre in 2019. It is the only unsubsidised theatre ever to be awarded the Channel 4 Playwrights Scheme bursary eleven times.

www.finboroughtheatre.co.uk

The Finborough Theatre has the support of the Channel 4 Playwrights' Scheme, sponsored by Channel 4 Television

The Finborough Theatre is a member of the Independent Theatre Council, the Society of Independent Theatres, Musical Theatre Network, The Friends of Brompton Cemetery and The Earl's Court Society, and supports #time4change's Mental Health Charter.

Supported by

The Finborough Theatre gratefully acknowledges the support for its 2019-2020 season from Bill Kenwright whose generous donation to the Finborough Theatre has made this year's work possible.

The FinboroughForum is supported by the George Goetchius and Donald Howarth Society of Friend's Awards.

THE FINBOROUGH THEATRE RECEIVES NO FUNDING FROM THE ROYAL BOROUGH OF KENSINGTON AND CHELSEA.

Mailing
Email admin@finboroughtheatre.co.uk or give your details to our Box Office staff to join our free email list.

Feedback
We welcome your comments, complaints and suggestions. Write to Finborough Theatre, 118 Finborough Road, London SW10 9ED or email us at admin@finboroughtheatre.co.uk

Playscripts
Many of the Finborough Theatre's plays have been published and are on sale from our website.

On social media

 www.facebook.com/FinboroughTheatre

 www.twitter.com/finborough

 finboroughtheatre.tumblr.com

 www.instagram.com/finboroughtheatre

 www.youtube.com/user/finboroughtheatre

Friends

The Finborough Theatre is a registered charity. We receive no public funding, and rely solely on the support of our audiences. Please do consider supporting us by becoming a member of our Friends of the Finborough Theatre scheme. There are four categories of Friends, each offering a wide range of benefits.

Richard Tauber Friends – David and Melanie Alpers. David Barnes. Mark Bentley. Kate Beswick. Deirdre Feehan. Michael Forster. Jennifer Jacobs. Paul and Lindsay Kennedy. Martin and Wendy Kramer. John Lawson. Kathryn McDowall.

William Terriss Friends – Paul Guinery. Janet and Leo Liebster. Ros and Alan Haigh

Adelaide Neilson Friends – Philip G Hooker.

THE WIND OF HEAVEN

A Play

by Emlyn Williams

samuelfrench.co.uk

MUSIC USE NOTE

Licensees are solely responsible for obtaining formal written permission from copyright owners to use copyrighted music in the performance of this play and are strongly cautioned to do so. If no such permission is obtained by the licensee, then the licensee must use only original music that the licensee owns and controls. Licensees are solely responsible and liable for all music clearances and shall indemnify the copyright owners of the play(s) and their licensing agent, Samuel French, against any costs, expenses, losses and liabilities arising from the use of music by licensees. Please contact the appropriate music licensing authority in your territory for the rights to any incidental music.

USE OF COPYRIGHT MUSIC

A licence issued by Samuel French Ltd to perform this play does not include permission to use the incidental music specified in this copy. Where the place of performance is already licensed by the PERFORMING RIGHT SOCIETY (PRS) a return of the music used must be made to them. If the place of performance is not so licensed then application should be made to the PRS, 2 Pancras Square, London, N1C 4AG (www.prsformusic.com). A separate and additional licence from PHONOGRAPHIC PERFORMANCE LTD, 1 Upper James Street, London W1F 9DE (www.ppluk.com) is needed whenever commercial recordings are used.

IMPORTANT BILLING AND CREDIT REQUIREMENTS

If you have obtained performance rights to this title, please refer to your licensing agreement for important billing and credit requirements.

THE WIND OF HEAVEN

First presented at the St James's Theatre, on 12th April 1945, with the following cast of characters:

DILYS PARRY	Diana Wynyard
BET	Megs Jenkins
MENNA	Dorothy Edwards
GWYN	Clifford Huxley
PITTER	Arthur Hambling
AMBROSE ELLIS	Emlyn Williams
EVAN HOWELL	Herbert Lomas
MRS LAKE	Barbara Couper

The play was directed by the Author

ABOUT THE AUTHOR

Emlyn Williams (1905-1987), dubbed "the Welsh Noël Coward", was one of the most successful actor-dramatists of the 1930s and 1940s. His greatest works, *Night Must Fall* and *The Corn Is Green*, were made into films starring Albert Finney, Bette Davis and Katharine Hepburn, and remain much revived. Williams' plays have twice been rediscovered by the Finborough Theatre – *The Druid's Rest* in 2009, and Blanche McIntyre's multi-award-winning production of *Accolade* in 2011, which subsequently transferred to St James Theatre. Williams was a pioneering LGBTQ+ figure, and his remarkable life began in a working-class family in North Wales, where he spoke no English until the age of eight and could barely read or write. Coincidentally, he lived much of his adult life in Dovehouse Street, a short walk from the Finborough Theatre.

SCENES

To
Diana Wynward

CHARACTERS

DILYS PARRY
BET, her servant
MENNA, her niece
GWYN, a boy of thirteen
PITTER
AMBROSE ELLIS
EVAN HOWELL
MRS LAKE

SETTING

The action of the play takes place in the living-room
of a manor house overlooking the village of Blestin,
in the mountains of Wales

TIME

The summer of 1856, soon after the end of the Crimean War

Scene One

The living-room of a manor house in the village of Blestin, in the mountains of Wales. A fine summer morning in 1856.

The house is old and mellowed; its rustic lines harmonize unobtrusively with the softer details of an educated woman's taste; flowers in pots and vases, books, old Welsh portraits and miniatures, cushions and rugs.

To the extreme right, a staircase facing, climbing almost from the footlights, leads to a landing opening off right, with a small window facing the evening sun, one corner overgrown with ivy. At the foot of the stairs, in the right wall, a door leading by a passage to the kitchen. Under the stairs, an alcove leading (to the right) to the dining-room. In the back wall, center, a large deep fireplace, and to the left, up two steps, the main door leading to the hall. When this main door is open (it opens into the room) the hall can be seen beyond. The hall projects (out of sight) to the left, as a porch which frames the front door of the house (unseen but often heard opening and closing). In the right of the hall (out of sight) a small window which can reflect a pattern of leaves on the back wall of the hall. In the left wall of the room, downstage, a large bay window forms a deep alcove; through the lace curtains there is a glimpse of a stone wall in the garden (high enough to hide people walking along the path behind it) and over it a corner of the wall and roof of the porch: the window faces the morning sun.

Between the fireplace and the main door, sideways to the audience, a screen. In the hall, a clothes-stand on which hang shawl, cloak and bonnet. Against the left wall, above the window, a grandfather clock; near the window, an old-fashioned Welsh harp, with beside it a music-chair. Facing the fireplace (its back to the audience) a sofa, with along its back a sofa-table, and in front of the table, a high-backed armchair. Against the side of the stairs, a desk, with beside it a desk chair. Downstage, right, facing left, a low-backed armchair. Downstage, left, near the window, a three-seated conversation-piece, with near it a stool.

To the right of the fireplace, in the right wall, hangs a large round mirror. The fireplace itself is shielded by a large firescreen. In the window, a small table with a pot of geraniums.

Three oil lamps, one on the sofa-table, one on the desk, one on a small corner table above the window.

DILYS PARRY *sits in the conservation-piece, looking out of the window, a saucer and full cup of tea beside her. She is a beautiful well-bred woman in her thirties, who would be more beautiful still if her expression were not so fixed and overcast; she wears a morning dress. She has little or no Welsh accent.*

The main door is open, and in the hall the sun streams in through the open front door.

A pause. The clock strikes eleven. A knock.

BET *enters from the kitchen, with brush and duster; she is a homely clean-looking Welsh peasant, between thirty and forty. Her Welsh accent is marked but not exaggerated.*

BET *(seeing* **DILYS***)* Excuse me... *(She crosses, takes up the cup and saucer, looks down at the cup, then at* **DILYS***, who has not moved, and shakes her head)*

MENNA *runs down the stairs, happy and hurried. She is a beautiful girl of twenty dressed in a summer dress and a hat. She has little or no Welsh accent.*

MENNA *sees* **DILYS***, catches* **BET***'s eye and stops abruptly.*

BET *shows her the cup of tea and goes back into the kitchen.*

MENNA *stands looking at* **DILYS***, then plucks up courage.*

MENNA Auntie. *(As* **DILYS** *does not move, louder)* Auntie!

DILYS *starts and turns slowly to her.*

DILYS Yes, my dear?

MENNA Are you feeling better?

DILYS Better? *(She rises, and walks restlessly to the fireplace)*

MENNA You work too hard. *(Putting on her gloves)* When you think this is the first morning for eight months that you have spent at home, and not in that stuffy old Barn Hospital! After all, Auntie, the war has been over for weeks, and Mrs Pugh the Top Hall heard from London that even the flags are put away.

DILYS *(rousing herself, smiling)* The war may be over in the Crimea, but down in our Barn, it still flourishes.

MENNA Mrs Pugh says it is wrong for a gentlewoman like you to dabble in such things.

DILYS *(sitting in the conversation-piece)* I suppose she thinks one Florence Nightingale is enough, without a local copy-cat.

MENNA *moves timidly.*

Where are you off to?

MENNA I came to ask your permission. Captain Isslwyn Pugh is home.

DILYS Mrs Pugh's boy? Home in Wales?

MENNA From the Crimea. And a Captain, with a wound in the foot.

DILYS (*smiling*) So that is why his mother is quoted at me! (*Amused*) So he has been pursuing you?

MENNA I'm afraid he has, Auntie. Through the Post Office.

DILYS (*quickly*) You thought I'd mind!

MENNA Twice a week, and when he was in danger, a scribble once a day. I have not slept much, Auntie... (*Kneeling to her, eagerly*) ...do you think it shows?

DILYS How did you know he was home, slyboots?

MENNA He came to his bedroom window and waved his shirt out of it.

DILYS His shirt?

MENNA He said his handkerchief would have looked better, but might not show. His letters are very amusing, at least I find them so.

DILYS Is he very dear to you?

MENNA (*after a pause*) I think of him day and night.

The smile fades from **DILYS**'*s face. She rises and walks to the window.* **MENNA** *watches her. Idly,* **DILYS** *plucks the strings of the harp, from one end to the other. The notes die away, thinly, sweetly. She looks round the room.*

DILYS This house is dead. Can you tell, Menna? (*Plucking the strings again, and looking round*) For a minute, you'd have sworn it was not dead, but listening. Did you notice? But not for long... Am I dead too? Wake up— (*Sinking onto the music chair*) —wake up!

MENNA If only you could talk about it!

DILYS *(looking at her, coldly)* Talk about it?

MENNA You never have, not since the day he died... There, I've said it! *(Kneeling, impulsively)* To you I'm a child, but let the tears flow—anything rather than this! Talk to me!

DILYS I'll talk to you. I'll tell you that for five years I was married to a fine man; a year ago next week, on his way home to me from the war, he died of the Crimean typhus; and the day after they told me, there died an unborn boy. That is all there is to say, that he is dead, and I can still breathe and think. And that new grief touches the heart of whoever is by, but old grief is irksome and wrinkles the face of the griever. *(After a pause, gently)* You mustn't be late, ymechani.

MENNA *rises and starts to go.*

Astride that stile sits your boy from Balaclava, his cap over one ear. Don't be late. *(She puts her hands suddenly to her face)*

MENNA *stands helplessly then runs out by the main door. The front door is heard closing behind her.*

A knock at the kitchen door: **BET** *enters, carrying an account-book.*

BET Escuse me, the washing-book.

DILYS *(collecting herself)* Thank goodness, work... *(She takes the book; she crosses to the desk for a pencil, and sits at the desk)*

BET Could I have a word, Mrs Parry, with all respect?

DILYS *(totting up)* What is it, Bet?

BET It's this man, Mrs Parry.

DILYS *(looking up)* Gracious, don't tell me you quiet mouse have been walking out too?

BET *(laughing)* No no—but you know about the man, that's the talk of the village?

DILYS But annwyl, I only see the postman, and I'm not in the habit of tea and tattle with him!

BET Well, this man is the one—with all respect, Mrs Parry, can I sit down for comfort to tell the story?

DILYS Do.

BET *(drawing up the high armchair, and sitting)* Well, he is the one that has took the room in the Blestin Arms, that never had anybody in the bed since old Mrs Williams Shop can remember—well, he has come and took it.

DILYS Who is he?

BET An English foreigner, but civil with it. And full of questions, so they say, like he was from the police.

DILYS The police?

BET Mrs Parry, with all respect—he is not after me, is he?

DILYS But why should he be?

BET Well, you know... *(Embarrased)* ...what we talk about when I first come to you, that you said you would not talk about again.

DILYS That? No, Bet, I promise you he won't be after you.

BET But Mrs Parry, could he be after Gwyn?

DILYS After a little boy? Gracious, why?

BET For not having a proper married couple for a father and mother.

DILYS But it's not his fault.

BET I know, but I heard say they are very touchy on it in the law courts. Quite right, granted, but—

A timid knock at the kitchen door. **DILYS** *goes back to her accounts.* **BET** *rises guiltily, puts back her chair and dusts it with her apron.*

DILYS Come in.

GWYN *enters, carrying a basket of logs. It is difficult to see his face; he looks a dreamy delicate-looking peasant boy of thirteen, shabbily but carefully dressed. He goes up in silence, and lays the basket near the fireplace.*

BET *is about to go, when there is a knock at the front door; she goes out into the hall and is heard opening the front door, as* GWYN *puts his hand shyly to his forelock and goes back into the kitchen.*

PITTER *(offstage)* Mrs Parry? Would you say Mr Pitter?

BET *(offstage)* Pitter...yes, sir.

She returns, agitated.

DILYS Pitter, did you say?

BET Quite right.

DILYS But it's nobody I know—

BET It is him, Mrs Parry.

DILYS The village Paul Pry? *(With an effort)* Ask him in. *(She rises)*

BET *looks at her uncertainly and goes back into the hall.*

This may liven up the morning...

BET *(offstage)* She says for you to come in.

PITTER *(offstage)* Oh, thank you so very kindly...

PITTER *appears in the doorway after handing his hat and stick to* BET. *He is a suave, spare Englishman of fifty, with pince-nez and careful black clothes. His old-maidish fussiness is a screen for great intelligence.*

Thank you so very kindly, Mrs Parry, and so distressingly early in the day, too, I hope I find you well, ma'am?

BET *edges apprehensively past him and hurries back into the kitchen.*

DILYS You don't look like a policeman.

PITTER The most passionate love letters I ever read, Mrs Parry, were penned by a governess with spectacles and a moustache... *(Pressing his breast)* What a climb—

DILYS *motions to the high armchair.*

Thank you so very kindly... Your Welsh hills may be joy to the eye, but they are torture to the feet.

DILYS Are you sorry you came?

PITTER *(looking at her quizzically, after a pause)* No. You see, Mrs Parry, I am before all else a student of human nature. Do you remember La Bruyère? By day he was humble tutor to the French nobility; at night he dissected them without mercy, with a quill pen. I rather fancy myself as La Bruyère. Will you allow me to ask one or two questions?

DILYS *(taken aback, sitting in the desk chair)* If you are from the police, I take it I have little choice—

PITTER Thank you so very kindly. This is your house?

DILYS It was left me by an uncle.

PITTER Delightful— *(Thoughtfully)* —then you have not always lived in this village?

DILYS No, I came here from England a year ago.

PITTER A year only—too bad...you are Welsh, of course?

DILYS Half-Welsh, yes. My mother's father was a farmer in this county.

PITTER Dear me, how charming... I learnt a good deal about you, of course, at the inn—

DILYS *(sharply)* I take no interest in the village, and I expect the same courtesy in return.

PITTER I beg your pardon... *(Rising, after a pause)* No interest in the village... Too bad. *(Looking out of the window, suddenly)* Are you religious, Mrs Parry?

DILYS Not at all. What made you ask?

PITTER There is no village church. I can understand there being no school, but there's no church either.

DILYS There hasn't been, for a hundred years. What used to be the church is now the shop.

PITTER Ah yes, the arch is still there. Interesting... *(Turning to her)* Mrs Parry, I am looking for a list of the inhabitants. But no church, no register. How am I to set about it?

DILYS I believe my uncle made it his hobby to keep account of local births and deaths.

PITTER Just the thing! Could you lay hands on it?

DILYS I'm not sure. *(Rising)* It should be in a bookcase in the dining-room—

PITTER *(picking up an open book from the arm of the high armchair)* Thank you so very kindly... *(Reading from the cover)* "The School of Spinoza". Yours?

DILYS Yes.

PITTER Can the philosophers give you the satisfaction they give me?

DILYS *(abruptly)* I'll look for your Domesday book.

She hurries into the dining-room.

PITTER *looks after her, puzzled; he crosses to the desk, puts down the book, and looks at other books.*

AMBROSE ELLIS *enters from hall. He is a flashily-dressed man in his thirties with top hat, oiled hair, gloves, rings and walking stick; his self-confident defiance lies like a lid over a cauldron of brooding nervousness. He speaks perfect English, but there is something temperamentally foreign about him. He advances laconically into the room.*

AMBROSE Good morning.

PITTER *(turning, with a start)* Good morning, sir. *(He goes tranquilly back to the books)*

AMBROSE No joyous bowings from the waist?

PITTER My only wonder, sir, is that you have not emerged from a trap-door with a flaming dagger in your mouth.

AMBROSE *(looking round the room)* An old-fashioned mode of entry, my dear Pitter, and in between trap-doors, difficult to live up to. *(Taking off his gloves, and tossing them on to the sofa)* I heard your voice and a woman's, and true to myself slunk inside for the pleasure of eavesdropping on the smack of lascivious lips. You've failed me, Pitter. *(Sitting in the high armchair)* A widow too.

PITTER A Mrs Parry.

AMBROSE She sounded plain and flat.

PITTER She has a cover of pride to her, very brittle, like egg-shell.

AMBROSE We'll see what we can do... *(Catching the other's eye)* That look, that quizzical gimlet, kindly turn it off! Those memoirs you are concocting, Pitter, I shiver when I think of them.

PITTER But what do my eyes say to you, sir?

AMBROSE They say "Stop being the man of the world, turn into yourself!"

PITTER And what is yourself?

AMBROSE That's the mischief. Take away the rings and the waistcoat, and what is there left? Sawdust. So let's flourish to the top of our bent...

AMBROSE *takes off his hat and hands it to* PITTER *who lays it on the table.*

Birmingham has sunk even deeper into the doldrums, so I thought I'd follow you up and see for myself. What was that about the police?

PITTER Everybody's first idea was that I must represent the law. It seemed a tolerable way of acquiring information.

AMBROSE Ha! We'll do this thing in style—what information have you?

PITTER None.

AMBROSE None? But isn't the countryside buzzing with it?

PITTER On the contrary. *(Sitting in the conversation-piece)* Did you come up through the village?

AMBROSE No, over the hill.

PITTER It is an odd village.

AMBROSE D'you mean unenlightened? Because these mountain hovels are each more brutish than the last—

PITTER No, unhappily one sees that anywhere—

DILYS *comes back from the dining-room, carrying an old ledger. She blows the dust from it.*

DILYS I'm afraid it may be out of date...

DILYS *sees* **AMBROSE**, *sitting like a magistrate.*

...oh.

PITTER *(who has risen punctiliously to his feet)* Mr Ellis, my superior.

DILYS I beg your pardon. *(Taking in* **AMBROSE**'s *clothes, with growing dislike)* I did not hear a door-knock.

AMBROSE There was none. I walked in without a by-your-leave.

DILYS Oh. *(She looks at* **PITTER***)*

PITTER *shrugs his shoulders, deprecatingly.*

How do you do?

AMBROSE Bursting with health.

DILYS I am relieved. I feared an infirmity of the lower limbs.

AMBROSE *(after looking at Pitter, twirling a ring)* When I was first flung into English society, with my stockings round my feet, I was forever bobbing up and down. I was in danger of bowing and scraping my way into obscurity. So I took to staying where I was. Planted in a chair, like a rude cabbage.

DILYS You must be much disliked.

AMBROSE I am happier disliked than ignored. Your book, please.

DILYS *stares at him, then at* PITTER, *who crosses, takes the book from her and places it before* AMBROSE.

(turning over pages) Births—deaths... Looks pretty comprehensive... Hallo. For the last three pages, no births are marked.

PITTER There have been no births, sir, since eighteen hundred and forty-five. Eleven years ago.

AMBROSE Strange... Why is Evan Howell underlined in red?

PITTER He is a farmer, and the nearest to a spokesman for the village. A man of some character, apparently.

AMBROSE We shall send for him. Shall I join the police force, what do you think? *(Studying the ledger)* Now...

DILYS What did you mean by that?

AMBROSE I am no more a policeman than you are.

DILYS Will you go, please?

AMBROSE No. *(Graciously)* Sit down.

DILYS Who are you?

AMBROSE *is about to answer, then motions to* PITTER.

PITTER Ambrose Ellis.

DILYS *(to* AMBROSE*)* I have never heard of you.

AMBROSE Are you sure?

DILYS Apart from an idea that Ambrose Ellis is a fairground in Birmingham, I have no—

AMBROSE Exactly. I am Ambrose Ellis.

DILYS You are the manager of a circus?

AMBROSE No no, that's *his* corner. *(Waving to* **PITTER***)* It amuses me to have my circus managed by an impoverished gentleman. I am the owner. *(Rising)* A showman.

PITTER A great showman.

AMBROSE *(taking the floor with a flourish of his stick)* Don't I look like a showman? Ain't I vulgar enough? Surely!

DILYS You are in one way, of course—

AMBROSE I should think so. But in another?

DILYS You speak too well.

AMBROSE Don't tell anybody, but I started out as a schoolmaster. Little Emrys Ellis, a Welsh pedagogue.

DILYS Welsh?

AMBROSE My ear catches with pleasure your note of surprise: I aim to give a vague effect of the Continent. *(Looking out of the window)* I was born not thirty miles from here, in darkness and in shame.

PITTER Mr Ellis returns home today, after twenty years.

AMBROSE Very touching, Pitter, but it is not my home. *(Turning to* **DILYS***, with an effort)* I am counting the hours till I return to Birmingham.

DILYS *(interested in spite of herself)* So you started out as a schoolmaster?

AMBROSE A little Welsh pedagogue in the red rosy hell of an English grammar-school. I was shorter then: I hadn't yet thought of stuffing the heels of my shoes with horsehair. The boys used to spit down my back. When one spat in my face, I felt the moment had come to feel humiliated.

DILYS What did you do?

AMBROSE Spat back and walked out.

DILYS *(sitting in the low armchair)* And bought some horsehair and turned from Emrys into Ambrose Ellis?

AMBROSE Precisely. *(Taking the floor again)* I fell in with a circus and started by tidying up after the elephants. Then like other small men before me, I read a book on Napoleon, and one wide-awake night vowed I would be rich and famous. Then I ran into my first bit of luck. A double-jointed young woman who told fortunes.

DILYS She performed acrobatics, and then foretold the future?

AMBROSE Not at all; both at once, by lying on her chest and holding in front of her eyes, between her toes, a tea-cup. I made five hundred pounds. Then I met a crossing-sweeper with three thumbs, and never looked back.

DILYS You put the poor thing into a circus?

AMBROSE Why not? It turned him from a poor thing into a rich one. No, I lead a full life, very amusing and deceptive.

PITTER Are you content?

AMBROSE *(turning)* Content?

PITTER Would you describe yourself, sir, as a happy man?

AMBROSE *(after a pause)* But contentment has never entered into it. I am violently busy, and devilish determined. *(Catching DILYS's eye)* And I have been clever enough to build a suit of armour for myself. *(He looks again out of the window)*

PITTER *(murmuring, thoughtfully)* Very brittle, like egg-shell...

AMBROSE What was that?

PITTER Nothing.

DILYS But what brings you to a remote village in a part of the world which you detest?

AMBROSE *(turning to her, and sitting)* That is where I must bully you into helping us.

DILYS Me?

AMBROSE Mrs Parry... *(Waving to* PITTER*)*

PITTER Mrs Parry, were you aware that in your remote village— *(Holding up the ledger)* —you harbour an exceptional human being?

DILYS Indeed?

AMBROSE You have no idea to what Pitter is referring?

DILYS Not the slightest.

> AMBROSE *and* PITTER *exchange a look.*

PITTER You at least know a tramp named Will Jenkins?

DILYS No... *(Taking the ledger)* Oh, wait a moment—something my servant said... *(Sitting in the high armchair)* Was he called before the Assizes for drunkenness and thieving?

AMBROSE He's the man.

> PITTER *searches in a wallet.*

He turned up in Birmingham, and being a criminal vagrant, decided that his natural port of call was my office. Next day this was sent round.

PITTER *(taking out a ragged paper)* Dictated, and just legible. *(Reading)* "For Circus, sir, you in Blestin village a magic little man you will find."

DILYS A dwarf, does he mean? With coloured scarves and rabbits?

AMBROSE No no, those are two a penny where we come from.

PITTER *(reading)* "He stand middle of a field, and two hands empty away off himself, music is heard in the air. Please ten pounds. I heard him."

DILYS On his way to, or from, the Blestin Arms?

AMBROSE *(rising)* That's what I asked myself. Then I detected a ring of conviction somewhere, and sent for him, to discover he'd had the impertinence to die of exposure during the night. Can you help us?

DILYS Not at all, except to assure you it's the figment of a fuddled brain. *(She takes the paper from* **PITTER***)*

PITTER I thought so at first, but those villagers are hiding something.

DILYS *(reading)* "Music is heard in the air."

PITTER Trickery or waves in the ether. *(He moves to the window and looks out)*

AMBROSE But can you conceive what this might mean to me? *(Pacing)* I can see the tent, gold trumpets, red flutes, and daubed right across, "Unique on Earth, Ambrose Ellis's Musical Dwarf". *(To* **DILYS***)* Introduce to me the village spokesman, this man... *(Pointing to the ledger)* ...Howell.

PITTER If you could only arrange for him to call here tonight.

DILYS *(after a pause)* Very well.

AMBROSE Ah... *(He goes to the sofa for his gloves and hat)*

DILYS You had better come to dinner first.

PITTER How very kind of you—and Mr Ellis?

DILYS Provided he behaves himself.

PITTER I will vouch for that. How very very kind of you. *(He looks out again)*

DILYS But why—when there may be money in this—why are the villagers making a secret of it?

AMBROSE Ah... Pitter has an answer to everything— *(Mockingly, smoothing his hat)* —speaking scientifically, Pitter, why are they hiding him?

PITTER *(after a pause, without looking round)* Half the slate roofs glistening in the sun, the other half in shadow. A Welsh village.

AMBROSE Or Irish, French, Scottish.

PITTER An ordinary mountain village... Before the Old Barn, the milkman stands with his pail for the military hospital. Two cart-horses heaving round the corner of the inn. Behind them, the shepherd—

AMBROSE *(impatiently)* No dwarfs?

PITTER Not yet... Now look, this is where this village is not like any other.

As **DILYS** *crosses to his side.*

Watch the shepherd and the smith.

DILYS *(looking, after a pause)* He passes him, without a look from one to the other.

PITTER Secret, sorrowful, And yet calm. As if they were waiting.

AMBROSE Waiting for what?

PITTER Even the sunlight seems to hang heavy between them.

DILYS *(thoughtfully)* And there are no children.

PITTER And suddenly, music is heard in the air.

AMBROSE *(after a pause, breaking a spell)* May a thirsty man of affairs remind his second-in-command that the village tap-room must be open? *(He puts on his hat before the mirror)*

PITTER I beg your pardon, sir, I was fancifying... Until this evening, Mrs Parry, and thank you profusely.

He kisses **DILYS**'*s hand, bows, and goes into the hall.* **AMBROSE**, *who has watched him in distaste, follows him to the main door, and turns to* **DILYS**.

AMBROSE *(in abrupt embarrassment)* Having no manners, madam, I get my manager to manage the hand-kissing for us both.

He bows awkwardly, and follows **PITTER** *out.*

DILYS *smiles, turns, and looks down at the village a moment, then round the room. She plucks idly at the harp, then sits in the conversation-piece as before; her mood of sadness descends on her again.*

BET *returns from the kitchen, with duster and brushes. She sees* DILYS *and hesitates.*

DILYS *(rising, with an effort)* Don't mind me, Bet. I'm going up to finish the linen.

BET Yes, Mrs Parry. *(She kneels, and begins methodically to brush the carpet)*

GWYN *comes in from the kitchen, carrying a stool and a box of cleaning materials. He sees* DILYS *and hesitates.*

BET *nods to him. He goes up, puts the stool down at the fireplace, stands on it, and polishes the ornaments on the mantelpiece.* DILYS *rouses herself, crosses and begins to walk upstairs.* BET *lets fall what she is holding, suddenly, and looks up, listening, an eager expectant look on her face.*

DILYS *(turning)* What is it?

BET I thought I hear something.

DILYS No, there's nothing.

BET That's right. There is nothing, thank you. *(She goes back to her cleaning)*

DILYS *starts to move again, then stops and looks at* BET, *puzzled. She waves aside her new thought, and hurries upstairs.*

The servant and her son continue their tasks.

The lights fade, and the curtain rises immediately on.

Scene Two

Evening of the same day.

The oil lamps are lit, though the window, curtains are still open to the growing darkness. On the table, a tray with coffee and cups. There is now a small table in front of the conversation-piece. The main door is closed. **AMBROSE** *sits on the conversation-piece, facing the window, a cup in his hand; he is deep in thought.* **PITTER** *stands at the low armchair, drinking coffee. A pause.*

AMBROSE I should have dressed.

PITTER I beg your pardon, sir?

AMBROSE I should have dressed, dammit. I'm not right in the evening without my tails and my paste-diamond tiepin.

PITTER I like our hostess. For a woman, she seems very intelligent.

AMBROSE I expect there's a catch somewhere.

PITTER I should like to have known her before he died.

AMBROSE Why?

PITTER We are meeting half of her, or less. One minute she is looking at you with the strained attention of the dreadfully bereaved; then you look again, and her eyes are as empty as glass.

AMBROSE D'you mean we oughtn't to be here?

PITTER No no, she welcomes the distraction. You amuse her.

AMBROSE Oh. I'm glad.

PITTER *crosses to the desk, taking a notebook from his pocket.*

Don't forget the strained attention of the dreadfully bereaved, that shouldn't look bad in print.

PITTER Exactly what I was thinking, sir. *(He writes)*

After a pause **AMBROSE** *puts down his cup on the small table, rises slowly, and looks down at the village. He closes the curtains abruptly and walks away.*

(writing) Are you feeling restless, sir?

AMBROSE More than restless, damn depressed. *(Sitting again)* I haven't had half enough to drink. I wish our man would come.

PITTER He should not be long.

AMBROSE I thought she was never going to light the lamps. *(Walking up and down, then stopping)* Ellis's Marvellous Musical Dwarf, in the Ambrose Ellis-ecum... No...

PITTER No good, excuse me, I must fetch my own pen... *(Rising)* On your honour, sir, you promise me not to look?

AMBROSE On my honour.

PITTER *goes into the hall.*

AMBROSE *crosses swiftly, takes up the notebook, and looks at it. He starts.*

PITTER *returns with a pen wrapped in baize.*

What d'you mean by this?

PITTER By what, sir?

AMBROSE *(reading)* "My little fellow" ...that's me, I take it?

PITTER It is, sir.

AMBROSE *(reading)* "My little fellow grows interesting. The more he feels the village... *(Looking up at* **PITTER**, *shaken, angry, then back at the book)* ...and hears deep in his bowels the rumblings of the spiritual volcano which is his true Celtic self, the more he plays the cynical braggart."

PITTER You promised not to look, sir.

AMBROSE You deserved what you got, appealing to my sense of honour. And I'd thank you to keep the less engaging portions of my anatomy out of your memoirs! *(He flings the notebook on to the desk, and sits glowering in the low armchair)*

PITTER *crosses to the desk, and sits, smiling.*

DILYS *enters from the dining-room, carrying a tray with bottle and glasses. She is wearing a more formal black dress.*

PITTER *rises.*

DILYS I beg your pardon, gentlemen, neither Bet nor I have the habit of drawing corks.

AMBROSE You should have come straight in, within a yard of me they pop of their own accord.

DILYS *(smiling, arranging glasses on the small table)* My husband always—always looked after those things...

A pause. The noise of the front door opening and shutting.

(quickly, brightly) Mr Pitter, pray return to your life-work.

PITTER *(bowing)* Thank you, ma'am.

AMBROSE Ha!

PITTER *returns to the desk.*

MENNA *runs in, in her cloak, flushed and out of breath. She stops as she sees the two men.*

PITTER *rises.*

DILYS Come in, my dear. Gentlemen, this is my niece Menna Parry. Mr Pitter and Mr Ambrose Ellis—Mr Ellis asks to be excused, his legs are bad. *(She pours two liqueurs)*

MENNA I am sorry, sir. *(She curtsies, takes off her cloak, then looks at **AMBROSE**)*

AMBROSE What are you staring at, madam? My legs?

MENNA I beg your pardon, but—are you the gentleman from a circus?

AMBROSE I am a circus.

DILYS Mr Ambrose Ellis is the Ambrose Ellis. *(She hands* PITTER *and* AMBROSE *a full glass each)* You remember, I told you this afternoon.

MENNA Isslwyn's mother just spoke of him too. *(She sits constrained for a moment, in the conversation-piece)*

AMBROSE *raises his glass to the light, sniffs the contents elaborately.*

DILYS *(taking* AMBROSE's *cup from the small table)* Is it satisfactory?

AMBROSE I haven't an idea. I'll drink anything out of a bottle, except ink.

DILYS *(to* MENNA, *as she puts the cup on the tray)* Did you have a good dinner, ymechani? Did Isslwyn see you to the gate?

MENNA To the door. *(Glowing with suppressed excitement)* I've never seen the village look like that.

AMBROSE Like what?

MENNA Grey, and thin, like gossamer. It looked as if it belonged to another world... *(She looks before her, happily)*

AMBROSE *rises restlessly, and walks up to the fireplace.*

DILYS *looks down at* MENNA, *touched, and kisses her head impulsively.*

I can't keep it to myself any longer, even with strangers here, I can't... Auntie Dilys, Isslwyn has asked me to marry him.

DILYS He has? Oh, 'fanwylyd I am so glad for you... *(Embracing* MENNA, *then calling, with her old gaiety)* She's young and happy—congratulate her, you two hard old hearts...

AMBROSE, *at the fireplace, raises his glass languidly, and sits on the sofa.*

PITTER It's charming, very charming... *(He goes back to his writing)*

MENNA It is not completely settled, of course—

DILYS But I'm delighted to give my consent, my dear—

MENNA I knew you would, Auntie Dilys, but—well, it's Isslwyn's mother.

DILYS Oh? But you have a little money—

PITTER *(half rising)* Would you prefer us to—

DILYS No no. *(To* MENNA*)* What is it, dear?

MENNA *(looking doubtfully at the others)* Well, I don't know—

DILYS Come, it can't be anything shameful if you've got the money! *(Going up to the table to pour coffee)* What is it?

MENNA Well, it is church.

A pause. PITTER *turns and listens.*

DILYS Church?

MENNA Isslwyn's mother wants you to go to church.

DILYS Me? But I haven't been inside a church for twenty years!

AMBROSE *turns and listens.*

MENNA Mrs Pugh knows that, and she says it looks odd.

DILYS *(pouring out a cup of coffee)* Considering that most people go three times every Sunday, of course it looks odd—it *is* odd! But it is surely my own affair.

MENNA *rises and turns away.*

I'm sorry, my dear.

PITTER I think, sir, perhaps we ought to go—

MENNA (*as* AMBROSE *moves thoughtfully down*) No, don't go, please, for a minute. (*Turning to* AMBROSE, *nervously determined*) —Mrs Pugh doesn't like you either.

AMBROSE What do I do, hang myself? (*He sits in the low armchair*)

DILYS (*laughing*) My dear Menna, you're forgetting your manners! What meddling ideas has Mrs Pugh been putting in your head?

MENNA It isn't only that, and Isslwyn says so too. (*Sitting, her determination crumbling suddenly*) Now I am making him sound stupid, and he isn't, he's fine and sensible—

DILYS You're young and very much in love, I would have behaved like you at your age—

MENNA Auntie Dilys, are you an atheist? (*A pause*)

PITTER This is interesting.

MENNA I'm not going to ask Mr Ellis, for I am *sure* he is one— but are you?

DILYS My dear, what an impossible question to answer! Atheism—these labels sound so fierce! How could it ever be as simple as that?

MENNA Mrs Pugh says, do you believe in God?

AMBROSE (*softly*) And Mrs Parry says...?

DILYS No.

MENNA (*shocked*) Oh...

DILYS (*coldly*) This is absurd, Menna, in a minute we shall be in the thick of a theological debate, and nothing in the world is more fruitless. Or dull. Have some coffee, it is still warm. (*She goes up to the table and pours out another cup, still holding her own in the other hand*)

PITTER (*rising*) But Mrs Parry, were you not elevated in the odour of the middle-class sanctity—were you not brought up in England?

AMBROSE Under the watchful eye of a good queen, and an even better Albert?

DILYS The last time I was inside a church I was fifteen. *(Giving* MENNA *her cup)* Sitting next to my grandmother, in an English town where she was feared by the entire congregation. The preacher... *(Hesitating and changing the subject)* ...another glass, Mr Ellis?

AMBROSE *(rising)* You are very kind...

DILYS *(sitting in the high armchair, and looking at the clock)* I left a message for Howell to be here soon after nine—

AMBROSE *(pouring)* But Mrs Parry, pray let us go back to your church—and its congregation, *revenons a nos moutons...* *(One foot on the conversation-piece)* The sermon was droning to its close?

DILYS *(drinking coffee)* Very slowly.

PITTER And your grandmother?

DILYS Grannie was snatching forty winks and at the same time keeping her chin in the air in a listening attitude: it was worth watching. Suddenly a door opened, there was a whisper in my ear. My mother, the only being who had ever loved me, was dying. I remember that I looked round, still stupid from the news. It seemed darker. The preacher eyeing the clock with a cough, and saying "Dear friends, I have other quarrels with the Calvinists". The ushers discreetly fingering their collection-plates. And in the pews, the rustle of black pockets delved into by white moneyed hands. I took a last look at the bland furtive faces, got up, and walked out into the heathen air of the street. I have never been back. *(A pause. She rises)*

(indicating the bottle) Mr Pitter?

PITTER *(thoughtfully)* No thank you kindly, ma'am—

MENNA But surely, Auntie Dilys, if you had believed in God, He would have given you strength to bear—

DILYS I have always had an open mind on the subject. Nothing has ever happened to fill it with the right thoughts, that's all. Now Menna, forget all the impertinent questions Mrs Pugh has asked you to trip me up with, and go to bed.

MENNA *hangs her head, and crosses to the stairs.*

DILYS *goes up and pours herself a second cup of coffee.*

MENNA *steps on the stairs.*

MENNA But couldn't you come to church, Auntie, just to show that—well, that all is well?

DILYS Exactly, Mrs Pugh is confusing being religious with being respectable. Go to bed, dear.

MENNA *(strained and obstinate)* She says if you turned your mind to God, you would be resigned to your widowhood.

A pause. **DILYS** *puts down her cup and looks at* **MENNA.**

DILYS "Resigned to my widowhood" ...I can hear her saying it... How dare she put into such a glib mouthful, what I have been feeling day and night for a year, how dare she? *(Restraining herself, roughly)* Go to bed.

MENNA *looks miserably from her to the others, and runs upstairs.*

(lightly) I must apologize, gentlemen. I hope I wasn't too harsh, the young can be irritating, though they don't mean it... *(Looking from one to the other, then round the room; then suddenly, uncontrollably, with a bursting cry)* My love, my love, where are you—where are you? *(The emotion of months pours out; she sobs wildly, indecently)*

AMBROSE *and* **PITTER** *rise, and stand helplessly by. A pause.*

I beg your pardon, gentlemen. *(Making herself recover)* Please believe that all this time I have not shed a tear, and I lose my balance in public. If I were a man, I could say, damn Mrs Pugh... I am deeply ashamed. I'll go walking in the garden, as a penance.

As **PITTER** *makes to move.*

Pray sir, don't disturb yourself— *(She moves towards the main door)*

AMBROSE *goes to the door, opens it slowly, and stands holding it, his eyes fixed thoughtfully before him.*

DILYS *passes him into the hall; as she is about to put on her cloak, there is a knock at the front door. She turns quickly, wiping her eyes.*

He's here—

AMBROSE I'll talk to him, you go your way—

DILYS I will not hear of it. It will teach me to indulge in hysterical display...

She disappears and opens the front door.

(offstage) Sut mai heno, Evan Howell?

EVAN *(offstage)* Da iawn, Mrs Parry—

DILYS *enters.*

DILYS Dewch ifewn, ag eisted-dwch...

EVAN HOWELL *appears in the main doorway. He is a tall striking-looking Welsh peasant of middle age, with a haggard spiritual face. He is poorly but neatly dressed, and has cleaned and brushed himself for the visit. He carries a battered hat. He looks uncertainly round the room.*

(indicating the high armchair) Eisteddwch yma— peidiwch a bôd yn swil—Mr Ellis and Mr Pitter, this is Mr Howell.

EVAN *(bowing)* Sut mai heno...

AMBROSE } *(together)* How do you do...
PITTER   }

DILYS *(indicating the wine)* Dyferyn o win, Evan Howell?

EVAN Dim diolch, Mrs Parry.

DILYS Mr Ellis, you were brought up in Welsh, would you favour us?

AMBROSE I repudiated my native tongue years ago.

DILYS Then the interview is going to be difficult. *(To* EVAN*)* Mae nhw'n siarad dim ond saesnig.

EVAN Wel, fedra'i gair neu ddau o'r iaith.

DILYS Yn wir? *(To* PITTER*)* He says he knows a little English.

EVAN *(slowly, like a child)* In my house there is a book.

DILYS Good. Eisteddwch i lawr, Evan Howell...

He sits stiffly in the high armchair. DILYS *follows suit, ceremoniously, and sits in the desk chair.* AMBROSE *shuts the main door and hurries to sit in the conversation-piece.* PITTER *stands near the foot of the stairs.*

EVAN In my house there is a book. English Bible Authorize Version it is, and in the night, when the daily toil in my farm is done, I commit the words to my heart. *(He has obviously hardly ever talked English in company before, and speaks with extraordinary clearness and simple dignity)*

AMBROSE *(putting down his glass and rising, the Napoleonic patron)* Now, my man—

DILYS Evan Howell, Mr Ellis is the manager of a menagerie.

PITTER The owner of a circus.

AMBROSE The position is roughly this, Howell—

EVAN Esgusodwch, fi, be-di circus?

DILYS *(turning to* AMBROSE*)* What is a circus?

AMBROSE Oh... A circus is... *(He gives up and waves to* **PITTER***)*

PITTER A circus is a place where tricks are performed by gentlemen, ladies, and animals.

AMBROSE I like that, Pitter, it has a dignified ring—

EVAN *(to him, interested)* What is your trick?

AMBROSE I own it. I have no trick.

EVAN You have an elephant?

AMBROSE Twelve. They run round biting each other's tails, to the tune of "Drink To Me Only With Thine Eyes".

EVAN Doth one stand on the back of the other?

AMBROSE No.

EVAN Oh...you have a lion?

AMBROSE Five. One very wild. He killed his keeper last February.

EVAN Doth one—

AMBROSE No, they don't stand on each other's backs, either.

EVAN Oh.

AMBROSE I have a parrot who can say "Rule Britannia" and "What's your game, Mr Gladstone?"

EVAN *(politely)* Nothing else?

AMBROSE *(lamely)* I have a— *(To* **DILYS** *and* **PITTER***)* —I hope I'm giving satisfaction?

EVAN Bear with me, sir...do you wish for me to shew myself in your circus?

AMBROSE You?

PITTER What is your trick?

EVAN I have always heard say that when the English behold somebody that is not English, they laugh very hearty. Lo, I would shew myself as a Welshman.

AMBROSE I'm afraid my public is a trifle too jaded for that. *(Eagerly, as* EVAN *rises)* But you could come as a keeper, a sort of companion—

EVAN No thank you, sir, I got my farm. I would fain thrust myself forward to convenant with ye for a sight of the circus—

AMBROSE *(grandly)* Any time, just mention my name—

EVAN I would indeed, if the elephants was to stand on each other's backs. *(Turning)* Nos da...

DILYS Evan Howell, Mr Ellis has heard something.

EVAN Something?

DILYS *(slowly)* Who is this creature who can make his own music?

EVAN *stares from* DILYS *to* AMBROSE. *A pause.*

PITTER Nobody will suffer—even if the little man is playing a trick.

AMBROSE What's more, there will be money in it, for you and for him. Come on, who is it?

EVAN *(after a pause)* The time is nearly come. But it is not yet.

DILYS *(quietly)* What do you mean, Evan Howell?

EVAN *(looking at* DILYS *steadfastly)* You are heavy in the heart.

DILYS *looks at* EVAN *with a start.*

(to the others) I have been thinking of Mrs Parry this day; all the time I was diggin' my field.

DILYS *(with an effort)* It is kind of you to be sorry for me, but please—

EVAN *(gently)* I am not sorry for you.

Everyone looks at EVAN.

And do you know why? Because great things are coming to you, Mrs Parry. Yea, the same great things that are coming to us all, in the village of Blestin.

DILYS Has the village of Blestin suffered?

EVAN Suffered...? *(Looking round at the others)* Ye have no heard. *(Turning to go)* Nos da.

DILYS Evan Howell!

EVAN *turns.*

After what you have just said to me, they have the right to know.

EVANS *hesitates, then moves back a step.*

EVAN Eleven years ago. In Blestin nothing we knew of the world, but we could plough and sow, and reap, and sing. Wickedness in plenty, but innocent wickedness; fights in the road, but games in the road as well, the same men playin' as fightin'. The singin' was the best.

DILYS *sits slowly, to listen.*

A man would start a song—not thinkin', just between the teeth—and lo, in twos and threes they come, and in half an hour the whole eight score and seven of us out in the road. All singin'. But the day came...when the young ones go down to Port Blestin, and take three sailing boats; three score and four boys and girls under ten, and twenty babes in arms, on the finest day of summer. Not a breath of the wind. But lo, in the corner of the sky, no bigger than a man's hand—and that is out of my book—a cloud. And it come to pass that the cloud grow to fill the sky with power, a storm like none of us in Wales hearken to; and the boats washed up next day, and the bodies one by one. My married girl and her two little ones, I find them myself. The few left in Blestin, they come to me: as pitiful as any of my own beasts when they got no comfort, and go draggin' their pain from one door to another. We have lost our children, I spake to them, in bitterness they have been torn from us; and in bitterness the men and the wives will stay from each other, there will be no more children in Blestin. And since the day the first poor swollen babe was cast ashore like a bladder of foul air, not a voice hath rose in harmony. Dead in our hearts we have been, like you are now, Mrs Parry. Dead as the proper dead in the ground.

A pause. **AMBROSE** *rises, abruptly.*

PITTER You talk of the bitterness of that time: but there is no bitterness in your voice as you tell of it.

AMBROSE What has happened to change you?

EVAN *(after a pause)* Something in the last seven years. Something in the air of Blestin.

AMBROSE Go on.

EVAN Like when that storm was goin' to break. Only this is no storm, but a wonder.

PITTER Music, for instance?

AMBROSE Played by a dwarf?

EVAN *(not understanding)* Excuse me—a dwarf?

DILYS Dyn bach, Evan Howell—

EVAN *(laughing, very amused, stooping and holding his hand a couple of feet off the floor)* Ah, a little man... Na na, our little man is not a dwarf.

PITTER One more question—what is this...wonder?

EVAN It is writ in my book at home. John five twenty-four. *(Going, then turning, and looking at* **AMBROSE**, *holding his hand again at a mannikin's height)* A dwarf...

He goes out by the main door, stifling his merriment.

AMBROSE I'm glad he's amused.

PITTER It's not a dwarf, but it's a little man.

AMBROSE *(coming down to the others)* The question is, is he going to be any good to me?

DILYS *(to him)* Will you be honest enough to say that for a moment your Welsh blood too, was tingling?

PITTER With something new?

DILYS Something—strange?

AMBROSE *(after a pause, abruptly)* The night air, I expect. We shall call on you in the morning—

He goes into the hall and takes down his overcoat.

DILYS What were the numbers he said?

PITTER The Gospel according to Saint John, fifth chapter, twenty-fourth verse.

DILYS *crosses to the kitchen.*

AMBROSE *(offstage)* Bravo, Pitter, the true pulpit manner—

DILYS *(opening the kitchen door, and calling)* Bet!

BET *(offstage)* Yes.

DILYS May I borrow your Welsh Bible a moment?

BET *(offstage)* Yes, Mrs Parry—

PITTER Now the tramp in Birmingham said—

AMBROSE *enters.*

AMBROSE *(buttoning his coat)* "In Blestin a magic little man you will find" ... *(He comes down and drinks the remains of his wine at the small table)*

DILYS A little man. A small creature...

PITTER Ah, a small creature? Why not a boy?

DILYS A little boy! Of course— "dyn bach" —a little boy!

AMBROSE But there are no children in Blestin.

DILYS *(perplexed)* Then what—

A footstep; thirteen-year-old **GWYN** *enters from the kitchen, carrying a small Welsh Bible. He goes to* **DILYS,** *gives her the Bible, touches his forelock timidly, looks round, goes to the sofa table, and collects coffee cups, saucers and glasses onto the tray.*

The others look from him to **DILYS**, *as she opens the Bible, searches, and finds what she is looking for.*

PITTER What is it in English?

DILYS *(translating slowly)* "The hour is coming, and is here, when the dead shall hear the voice of the Son of God. And they that hear, shall live."

She looks at **AMBROSE**; *he looks at her. The child crosses to the kitchen, carrying the tray.* **DILYS**'s *eyes follow him.*

The lights fade, and the curtain rises immediately on.

Scene Three

Early the next morning; the window curtains are almost closed; through a narrow gap between them the morning sun fills the room with a faint light. The main door is closed. On the table, a tray with coffee utensils; the small table has been removed with the wine.

DILYS *comes slowly downstairs. She is in the same black dress, with over it a dressing-jacket. Caught in the shaft light, on the stairs, she stands a moment and surveys the eerie stillness of the room. She comes down, walks across, and stops as she sees the Bible on the conversation-piece, open at the same page as before. She picks it up, and stands looking at it in the half light.*

A knock at the front door.

She looks up, surprised, goes up into the hall, and is heard opening the front door.

DILYS *(offstage)* Mr Pitter!

PITTER *(offstage)* Oh thank you, so very kindly—

He enters in his overcoat, out of breath and, for him, perturbed.

I beg your pardon—a call before breakfast—so very irregular. How fortunate that you should be already abroad—would you be so good as to call the young lady?

DILYS Menna?

PITTER It's a trifle urgent. It— *(Sitting; abruptly)* —I'll explain when I recover my breath.

DILYS *looks at him, puzzled, then goes to the stairs.*

DILYS *(calling)* Menna!

MENNA *(offstage, startled)* What is it?

DILYS Finish dressing quickly, dear, will you?

MENNA *(offstage)* Yes—

DILYS *(coming downstairs)* What is it?

PITTER I happened to be the only one stirring, and the hospital doorman seized on me.

DILYS The hospital?

PITTER It is to do with young Pugh.

DILYS Menna's young man?

PITTER It appears that, on his mother's insistence, he was taken in an hour ago. *(Rising, panic-stricken)* And he saw your niece to the door last night—the picture of health!

DILYS You mean—

PITTER The plague. The Crimean plague.

DILYS The typhus? Nonsense, typhus takes a full day to develop—

PITTER It is still the plague. *(He sits again)*

DILYS Why, Mr Pitter! What's this? You, the rational philosopher, saddling the old scare-word of "plague" and riding it for all it's worth!

PITTER *(abruptly)* I dislike talking about death.

DILYS Only a monster would enjoy it—

PITTER I dislike it specially and intensely.

DILYS *(thoughtfully)* Go on.

PITTER I will go three streets out of my way to avoid a dead cur in the gutter. I have never seen a dead human being, and never intend to... *(Rising, and seeing the Bible)* Have you seen the boy since we left you?

DILYS No.

PITTER Or his mother?

DILYS Not yet.

MENNA *hurries downstairs, buttoning a wrist.*

MENNA Auntie Dilys, what is it? But it's only just morning—

DILYS I'm sorry to have startled you, annwyl, it's probably nothing. It's your fiancé.

MENNA My fiancé? Oh yes... I'm sorry, I did not think what you meant—

DILYS He has been taken suddenly poorly, that is all, and has asked to see you.

MENNA Asked to see me...but he was perfectly well—

PITTER It appears you will be allowed to wave to him through the window of the ward—

MENNA The ward? Is he in hospital?

DILYS I assure you it's only a precaution—

MENNA Is it—the plague from the war?

DILYS Of course not. A feverish cold, I expect, and his mamma's imagination has done the rest.

She goes into the hall, as MENNA *sits, and returns with* MENNA*'s cloak.*

It will do him good to see you, even through a dirty pane of glass—

PITTER *(going to the hall)* I have Mr Ellis's conveyance outside, I could deposit the young lady at the gate.

DILYS Thank you.

PITTER *exits.*

MENNA *(to* DILYS*)* I promise you I'll be sensible. Is he in danger?

DILYS If I thought he was, would I be staying behind?

She kisses MENNA, *who makes to go, then turns to her.*

MENNA I'm glad you said fiancé, even though it's a word I can't pronounce.

She hurries after **PITTER**, *who leaves the front door open.*

DILYS *stands thinking for a moment, then sees the harp near her. She strikes a chord, as she did before. The notes sound timidly through the room, and die away. The room is still and silent.*

DILYS *crosses and starts to go upstairs. She hears the click of the kitchen door, and stops.*

BET *comes in from the kitchen, carrying a long-handled broom; she leans the broom against the armchair, crosses, and opens the window curtains. The room is flooded with sunlight.* **BET** *turns and sees* **DILYS**, *with a start.*

BET Oh! Beg pardon, Mrs Parry, you give me a bit of a fright.

DILYS I'm sorry. It's early, isn't it?

BET Just turned seven. *(She suddenly notices that* **DILYS** *has not changed her clothes, and stares)*

DILYS What is it, Bet?

BET Mrs Parry, escuse me...you have not been to bed?

DILYS *(looking down at her dress)* No. I felt restless. I came down twice and made myself some coffee.

BET *(seeing the cups)* Oh yes—I am sorry, Mrs Parry fach, if you have been grievin' again.

DILYS I wasn't grieving exactly. Just...restless... *(She comes down and crosses slowly towards the window)*

BET *(collecting the cups on the tray)* Oh, I am sorry.

DILYS I found what I wanted in your Bible.

BET Thank you. *(She takes up the Bible from the conversation-piece and puts it casually on the table)*

DILYS *watches her narrowly.*

(feeling DILYS's *eyes still on her and turning)* Shall I come in and dust in a minute, eh, and make you a bit of a cup of tea this time—

BET *takes up her broom and starts to go.*

DILYS *(abruptly)* Where is your son?

BET Gwyn? He is down the garden, by the tree that fell down, choppin' my wood for me. Anyways, he was... *(Peering out of the window)* Yes, there he is.

DILYS *(looking)* Oh yes...

BET Did you want him, Mrs Parry, to go on a message for you?

DILYS No, no.

BET Thank you, Mrs Parry. I will pour you a good cup of tea.

She goes back into the kitchen.

DILYS *stands without moving, looking out at the boy.*

AMBROSE *walks in by the open front door, and stands in the doorway. He wears the same outré overcoat, with under it a more sober suit; he carries his hat in his hand. He looks as aggressive as before, but there is an air of strain, of mental conflict, about him; his eyes are marked with sleeplessness. He looks slowly round the room, and walks down smartly till he faces* DILYS.

She hears his footstep, turns, and faces him.

AMBROSE We said we'd sleep on it. Well?

DILYS I didn't sleep. Did you?

A pause. There is between them an unconscious air of conspiracy.

AMBROSE There's a light in your eye that wasn't there yesterday.

DILYS Is there? *(Guardedly)* It's the novelty, perhaps, of something to puzzle over.

AMBROSE Puzzle?

He hangs his hat in the hall and returns.

I'm not puzzled.

DILYS No? What are you so sure about?

AMBROSE My procedure for the rest of today. I've got to draw this little musical critter under my wing before any of those circus sharks get him into their clutches.

DILYS Under your wing?

AMBROSE If you prefer it, before they draw him under their wing I want to get him into my clutches. If he can produce music out of nowhere, I'll do ditto with the sovereigns. And there's every chance that if he— *(He sees out of the window, and stops)*

DILYS *(looking past him)* I had never noticed him before. *(Softly)* He is cutting wood. For his mother, who is my servant.

A pause. **AMBROSE** *turns; their eyes meet.*

What were you thinking?

AMBROSE *(sitting, abruptly)* That he's a real boy all right, which will make him more appealing to my public.

A pause.

DILYS *(suddenly)* I cannot get it out of my mind...

AMBROSE My dear Mrs Parry—

DILYS You were moved too, last night!

AMBROSE You were moved, were you? Shall I remind you of your words as I left? "You are a man of affairs," you said to me, "and I am a woman who has not been inside a church for twenty years and prefers to use her reason. In the morning"

—you said— "we shall be smiling indulgently at the whole business."

DILYS *(thoughtfully, carefully)* When that door closed behind you both, it was silent in the house. Suddenly, I heard a sound. The beating of my own heart. And I knew that this house is dead no longer. I spent the night walking from one window to another; it has been like a war inside me. One side shouted "You are a sensible woman who has stumbled on a small myth in Blestin, Wales, that has grown out of a great myth in Palestine, Asia."

AMBROSE And your other side?

DILYS The other side whispered, "Put away your philosophies, what comfort have they brought us? Let your heart beat to the full, for great things are in the making."

AMBROSE *(sharply)* Is that reasonable?

DILYS No. And that may not be a bad thing, either. The only other time I lapsed from reason, I was alive.

AMBROSE Your husband, you mean?

DILYS And last night I felt reason...slipping away from me again. I looked out at the sky. It was holding its breath. The silence was watching me, and saying "So *you know?*" Ambrose Ellis, is something come to us that for two thousand years the tear-stained blood-sick world has been waiting for? Is Jesus coming to Blestin village?

A pause.

AMBROSE *(in a dry, controlled voice)* The sun is up, and there's another day of bargaining started, bargaining for a place in that sun. Apart from the birth-pangs and the death-pangs, there's nothing I hear much, but the bargaining... And the rumour of the Crimean plague. From what Pitter told me on the road just now, that is one thing that may easily have come to Blestin. Blestin, the village of the religious mania. A mania to which a Mrs Parry is tempted to yield, as a desperate remedy for sickness of mind. Those are the facts. I like facts. They keep one sober.

DILYS *(holding his wrist a moment)* Is that why your pulse is twice the normal speed?

As he looks down hastily.

Do not forget I am a nurse.

AMBROSE Don't you think I may be excited too, at the prospect of a unique business deal? I shall bring it off sooner if you coax this emotional bee out of your bonnet.

DILYS *(relaxing, smiling)* It is hard to believe you have been a schoolmaster. I will obey you, sir, and—smile indulgently at the whole business.

She sits in the conversation-piece.

AMBROSE Good... *(Eagerly)* Now—will you do one thing for me? Talk to the mother.

DILYS I have an idea that may not be so easy—

A knock at the kitchen door.

BET *enters and hands* **DILYS** *a cup of tea as* **AMBROSE** *goes into the hall, taking off his overcoat and hanging it up.*

BET *(seeing him)* Shall I get the gentleman some breakfast, Mrs Parry?

DILYS Thank you, Bet, not just yet.

As **BET** *crosses to go back.*

Gwyn gets up very early, doesn't he?

BET I don't believe in coddlin' a boy that age.

AMBROSE *returns and listens.*

DILYS How old is he?

BET Fourteen his next birthday.

DILYS When did you first come to me, Bet?

BET A year next month, Mrs Parry.

DILYS What exactly did you do before then?

BET *(startled, looking at* **AMBROSE***)* Oh...but escuse me, Mrs Parry, I told it all to you, and you said all right—

AMBROSE turns away and sits on the sofa facing the fireplace.

DILYS Of course it was all right, Bet—but I wasn't paying attention. *(Drinking)* You lived in the village, did you?

BET In Blestin, yes. Housekeeper to old James Jones Shoemaker I was, and then two years last August we buried him. I told you—

DILYS But how did you both live after he died?

AMBROSE turns his head and listens.

BET After he died? Gwyn and me made ourself free-an'-easy, and we went back to live in the pigsties.

DILYS The pigsties?

BET Oh, no pigs, Mrs Parry, we wasn't as free-an'-easy as all that...! We had a good day clearin' the sties out, the two of us, never off of our knees, and Gwyn makin' me laugh the way boys will, snortin' behind my back so I was gospel certain the proper tenants were home again. But by the time the sun was down, we got the place so it was better. It smell terrible homely, but no worse.

DILYS Were they very kind to you in the village?

BET *(after a pause, quickly)* I never did no beggin', escuse me, Mrs Parry.

DILYS I'm sure you didn't—

BET *(guardedly)* The only thing I ever took was boots. They was too big for him, but anything better than barefoot. Like one o' them gipsies. I would feel bad to see him barefoot... I take your tray. *(She goes to the table, sees the Bible, picks it up and lays it on the coffee tray)*

AMBROSE *rises, and walks slowly down.*

DILYS Thank you for lending me your Bible.

BET Pleasure, Mrs Parry. *(She takes up the tray)*

DILYS But how did you learn to read?

BET I cannot read, Mrs Parry, no time for that; but Evan Howell he read out of his English Bible, and I mark the side in my Welsh one, so now I know in my heart some of it.

DILYS What do you think of it?

BET *(ingenuously)* It is nice when it tell a story.

AMBROSE The life of Christ?

A pause.

BET *(moving away)* Yes, sir, it is a nice story that. I will be gettin' back to my work.

AMBROSE *(following her)* It seems a pity your son can't learn English, if he's to get on in the world.

BET He seems happy wi' the Welsh.

AMBROSE *(suddenly)* Is he musical?

BET Musical, sir? No ear for a song at all, he is no Welshman there.

AMBROSE Do you want him to get on?

She looks at him for the first time, simply and steadily.

BET If he is to get on in the world, sir, I am willing. I am willing for him to do whatever it is right for him to do.

She goes back into the kitchen. A pause.

AMBROSE *(brusquely)* You were right, dammit; it isn't easy. I was hoping for another sort, the garrulous mamma of the child genius. This is the Welsh peasant with a vengeance, thrifty and cautious. She knew what we were after.

DILYS It's deeper than caution: you could see she was unprepared, yet she was as honest as the day. But more than anything... curiously ill at ease, did you not notice? As if we were prying into details of a secret life.

She rises, thoughtful, inwardly excited. A pause.

AMBROSE She's heard about the circus, and she's biding her time... Is it any good my talking to *him*?

DILYS Having gone to such pains to unlearn your Welsh, how can you?

AMBROSE *(nettled)* You could question him.

DILYS *(looking again out of the window)* I suppose so.

AMBROSE Will you?

DILYS Not yet.

AMBROSE Why not?

DILYS I don't quite know... Yes, I do. I'm afraid to.

AMBROSE Afraid because you know it would burst the balloon?

DILYS Perhaps...

As AMBROSE *sits in the high armchair, rubbing his eyes.*

Did *you* sleep at all last night?

AMBROSE I went walking, a practice I have detested for years.

DILYS Where did you walk?

AMBROSE Up this mountain. I had not been alone on a mountain since I was a child.

DILYS Your Welsh childhood... *(Sitting)* And last night that childhood came back to you?

AMBROSE *(after a pause)* I used to spend hours by myself, squatting barefoot on the edge of a crag, with the wind for company. A little ugly goat.

DILYS But your little mind was not the mind of a goat.

AMBROSE No, my mind had wings... *(Realizing what he has said, and meeting her eyes, speaking roughly)* Sounds fanciful, does it? Well, it happens to be true. I could feel it—positively feel it, I tell you—first beating inside my breast, knocking feverishly against the bones...and then out, away. High— wide...away. I held out my hands after it, they glowed in the dark. I was part of the earth, I was part of the sea and the sky—I was alive! Once, in the adoration of the moment, my body tried to strain after my mind, and I was on the point of crashing to a ridiculous death.

DILYS And if you had?

AMBROSE I'd have been lowered hastily into a pauper's grave by the crossroads; and the grave, on the small side, being a child's, would be forever mistaken for a dog's.

DILYS But something at least little Emrys had achieved. He had filled the earth and the sea and the sky with the glow of his own spirit. Can you say the same of big Ambrose, that has his name in letters of flame across a dozen tents, stitched there by a hundred underpaid sempstresses?

AMBROSE No, not the same. Last night it might have been the same mountain; I looked at my hands. *(Looking at them)* Larger, more worn, manicured: but jutting from the same body, flowing with the same blood. This body of mine, I thought, this shell I must cart about to the end of my days... what has it been up to, all those years in between? Eating, drinking, making money, and making love. More money than love—and better quality too. *(Meeting her eyes, and rising. Naïvely, at a tangent)* I've got a lot of money, did I tell you? Thirteen thousand pounds in this new Lancaster and Carlisle railway stock—they say it can't fail to rattle up—three thousand cash in case of national emergency, four rows of mansions in the best residential quarter of Birmingham, and three public houses in the worst.

DILYS *(smiling)* But the mountain, last evening... You suddenly felt weary of your body?

AMBROSE Sick to the point of nausea. Somewhere a donkey brayed, and I was reminded of my circus, my smelly squabbling sham of a circus. I started to count up figures. And I realized that far from being a bird, my mind was like that donkey, tied to a tread-mill, plodding blindly round. And round.

DILYS No adoration.

AMBROSE Adoration?

DILYS You used the word just now. You, the child Emrys, were filled with adoration. Do you realize, my friend, what we are on the brink of?

AMBROSE What?

DILYS A topic that in every church, and in most moneyed households in the land, rolls so glibly off every tongue, that it has worn away all its strangeness and its terror. We are on the brink of religion.

A pause.

AMBROSE Two restless fools, waiting for a miracle when the age of miracles is past...

DILYS A miracle?

Scarcely daring to, they look at each other.

A soft rap at the open front door.

AMBROSE *(rising, jocularly, breaking his own mood, and DILYS's)* Ah, Pitter. I know that knock! *(Walking up to the hall)*

PITTER *appears in the hall, absently putting down his hat and stick, and* BET *goes up unobtrusively from the kitchen to the dining-room, carrying a breakfast tray.*

Monsieur La Bruyère, quick! The end of your walking-stick, we are waist deep in a morass of speculation!

PITTER *advances into the room.*

You're thoughtful, Pitter. *(Bantering)* Do the villagers still look as if they were waiting?

PITTER Every time I looked round, they were looking round at me.

AMBROSE *and* DILYS *exchange a look.*

DILYS Would you say they were uneasy?

PITTER No, very serene. With a sly sudden glitter of excitement. Very odd.

AMBROSE *(coming down to him)* Is this child going to be any good to us, or isn't he?

PITTER Ask his mother. *(He looks searchingly at* AMBROSE*)*

AMBROSE *quails before the look, then dismisses it.*

AMBROSE The oracle has spoken. And this time, Mrs Parry, there must be no innuendoes. I've got to know where I am.

DILYS I will not allow you to be unkind to her.

AMBROSE *(moving vigorously to the kitchen)* I can't vouch for my temper, but I'll try— *(He hears a sound in the dining-room)*

BET *enters.*

BET *(timidly)* Escuse me— *(She makes to go to the kitchen)*

AMBROSE *steps forward and faces her. She stops, looks from him to the others, and turns pale.*

AMBROSE I am going to ask you one or two questions.

DILYS Bet, there's nothing to worry about—

AMBROSE Very simple questions.

BET *(hardly above a whisper)* Yes, sir. *(She twitches with tight fingers at her apron)*

AMBROSE *sits in the desk chair, and faces her.*

AMBROSE It's about your son.

BET Yes.

AMBROSE Did you foresee that he would be the subject of this inquiry?

BET Yes, sir.

AMBROSE *(startled)* Why?

BET I—I—

DILYS Speak your mind, Bet, don't be frightened—

AMBROSE What made you so sure?

BET *(blurting it out)* I will tell you, sir, and not the spit of a lie. I am worried about the way people in this part of the world are carryin' on about him.

DILYS You mean—praising him?

BET *(eagerly)* They are making him out to be something that no ordinary boy could be.

PITTER You mean—

BET I mean what it say in the Gospel of John. There, I have said it...

DILYS *sits in the conversation-piece.*

Oh, what you have lifted off of my poor chest, a house and the furniture!

AMBROSE But when did this idea start?

BET Soon after we come to Blestin, sir.

PITTER When was that?

BET Seven years ago. Six he was.

AMBROSE Where did you live before then?

BET Glantos, sir, by the sea. At peace there we was, and him a healthy babby, and nobody so much as look at me, but in Blestin... (*Suddenly distressed and loquacious*) Every time we go down the road, there they are behind their windows, stare, stare, people did ought to keep themselves to themselves, indeed they ought!

PITTER But where did this extraordinary idea come from, about your son?

BET From the music, sir.

A pause.

AMBROSE Ah...

BET Just a bit of music.

AMBROSE Never mind how ordinary it was—how did you first hear it?

BET *looks at* **DILYS** *entreatingly.*

DILYS (*to* **BET**) Don't be afraid, Bet.

BET It was the morning. And the spring of the year, because the trees that been black spikes for so long you could hit them for it, was by now green bubbles all over them. (*Awkwardly*) We was in the pigsties by then...

AMBROSE *stares at* **BET** *and she is overcome with shyness.*

DILYS (*rising and bringing forward the high armchair*) Sit down, Bet, for comfort to tell your story.

BET (*gratefully*) Thank you, Mrs Parry... (*Sitting*) I was stoopin' just outside the door, over our bit of washin' —

PITTER Wait a minute—what exactly was in your mind at that moment?

AMBROSE (*drawing his chair up to* **BET**'s) What were you thinking?

BET I wasn't thinking, sir, or doin' any such harm at all.

PITTER What sounds could you hear?

BET Very homely, to start with. You know the sad life there has been, in this village? Well, a clank of the horse-shoe, but no song from the smith: a rattle of the pail of the milk, but no song from the milkman... An' all of a sudden, of a bright quiet spring morning, standing by our pigsty, I heard it.

DILYS The music?

BET At the first, I think for sure it is noises in my head, and I just goin' to blow my old nose, to help...when it come to me that it is not in my head.

DILYS Was it singing?

BET Like men and women, you mean? (*Her eyes closed, trying to recall*) No, not singin'. More like a wind.

A pause.

PITTER Was it like musical instruments?

BET Escuse me, sir?

PITTER Clarionet, pianoforte, violoncello?

BET (*after indecision*) Could you fall back into the English?

PITTER Was it like this? (*He strikes the harp, vigorously*)

BET (*discouraged*) I don't know, sir, like a wind, I am sorry...

A pause. **AMBROSE** *rises and crosses, thoughtfully.*

DILYS Where did it come from?

BET (*suddenly sure*) It was everywhere.

AMBROSE How do you mean, everywhere?

BET The sky, and the earth that my two feet was on, and the air that is between. (*Losing her fear, in simple wonder*) It catch the little things best, like the proper wind does: the bit o' white cloud that you get in the spring, blowin' past the mountain there, and the tip of the tres, wi' the green bubbles on 'em.

DILYS Was it a sorrowful sound?

BET Sorrow? It was happy.

DILYS How happy?

BET *(after a pause, concentrating)* It was like as if you was to take all the children in Wales, an' tell them they can stay up an' play until they drop, so long as they stand in a row just for now, and sing for joy: and then you take the song and give it to the sky to sing instead. Happy like that it was.

AMBROSE And he?

DILYS Where was he?

BET Coming across the field, up to his knees in the grass, for he then was six years old. Cap on the back of his head, like boys get when they been running, isn't it—but walking very slow he is now, with the sun on him, slow as if it was for the comfort of the little thing he is carryin'.

DILYS What was that?

BET A lamb.

AMBROSE *(stiffly, after a pause)* A lamb?

BET Such a babby that it wasn't able to walk. And he was carrying it, you see, for me to have a look. And with him coming to the stile, he jump over, lamb and all, and I shout at him quite nasty "Put down that beast," I say, "with it being Evan Howell Farmer's do you want you and your Mam in jail for sheep-stealin'?" *(Realizing she is talking too much, rising)* Please can I go?

AMBROSE But the music?

BET With gettin' worried about the police, I did not notice it was finish.

PITTER *(after a pause)* And you call that ordinary?

BET Well, sir, if it happen, it must be ordinary, isn't it?

AMBROSE Bravo! Mrs Parry, your philosophers are beaten at their own game! Now more commonsense—what did he say when you spoke of the music?

BET I never did mention it, sir.

PITTER You didn't?

BET Not to him, sir. I thought it make him feel awkward.

AMBROSE But you told others?

BET When Evan Howell ask about the lamb, I tell him. And sorry I am now, for he tell the others, and that is how it start.

PITTER They heard the music too?

BET Yes.

AMBROSE How often?

BET Sometimes twice in a week, then not for a month.

AMBROSE *(an attempt to be the business man again)* Can he produce this music to order?

BET I do not know, sir, I never interfere... Can I go now, sir, my kettle will be on the boil for Mrs Parry's breakfast—

AMBROSE Before I return to Birmingham, you and I and your son are going to have a little talk, which may prove strongly to your advantage.

He goes into the hall for his overcoat.

BET *(puzzled, polite)* Thank you, sir... *(Starting to go, then struck by a thought)* Escuse me, sir, did you say Birmingham?

AMBROSE *(offstage)* I did.

BET Is your name Ellis?

AMBROSE *(offstage)* It is. Ambrose Ellis.

BET And you own a circus?

AMBROSE *(offstage)* I do. You have doubtless heard of it.

He comes back into the room, buttoning his overcoat.

BET No, but Gwyn tell me about you. Excited he was! From a circus, he said, and all the way from Birmingham!

AMBROSE *(patronizing, as she turns to go)* I take it there was a good deal of chatter in the village last night, about my having arrived?

BET Oh, it was not last night that he told me! *(Going)*

DILYS When was it?

BET *(pondering)* Oh...it was the day he was on the mountain that long I thought sure he would not be back by the New Year... That's right, New Year Eve! The only thing is, he got the name wrong. Emrys Ellis, he call you.

She looks from one to the other, a little puzzled, and goes into the kitchen.

DILYS That was five months yesterday... *(To* PITTER*)* When was it the tramp first told you the name of this village?

PITTER Last Wednesday. Six days ago.

He and DILYS *look at* AMBROSE. *Struck with amazement and fear, he does not dare to look at one or the other; he walks abruptly into the hall, and out, as.*

The curtain falls slowly.

Interval

Scene Four

Some hours afterwards: early evening. DILYS *stands at the window, looking out. The main door is open.*

A knock at the kitchen door.

BET *comes in, wipes her hands on her apron, and starts to go upstairs.*

A knock at the front door.

BET *crosses into the hall, and lets in* PITTER.

PITTER *(offstage)* Good afternoon.

BET *(offstage)* Good afternoon, sir.

She hangs up PITTER's *hat, crosses, and goes upstairs.*

PITTER *comes into the room, carrying a packet of letters. He watches* DILYS.

PITTER Is Mr Ellis still there?

DILYS Sitting on the pile of logs now. And deep in the same frightening trance he's been sunk in since he walked from this room.

PITTER *(walking down, and peering past her)* Is that a tray beside him? From here it appears untouched.

DILYS It is untouched.

A pause.

PITTER *(sitting in the conversation-piece)* Where is the boy?

DILYS *(dreamily)* He went to market early, but should be back... *(Rousing herself, sitting on the stool, as)*

PITTER *takes out his notebook and writes a word in it.*

Monsieur La Bruyère, how go the epigrams?

PITTER *(writing)* They will have to be expanded. This week is proving more interesting than I bargained for when I arranged it.

DILYS *(surprised)* You arranged it? But surely your lord and master—

PITTER He sent me: I saw to that. He also followed me: I saw to that too. The tramp in Birmingham had told me exactly what was brewing in this village, and I was curious to see how my little emancipated Celt would behave.

DILYS *(smiling)* You must find it very comfortable, travelling the world in a kind of intellectual sedan-chair.

PITTER I used to be smug about it.

DILYS So this week is making a difference to you too?

PITTER Not a very satisfactory one, for it is jolting the sedan without unseating the contents.

DILYS How is it jolting you?

PITTER *(thoughtfully)* It is showing me a man I have known for many years, torn in two with as much agony as a saint upon the rack. It is making me—wonder... Oh, when I called for our letters from Birmingham, I found one for you.

DILYS *(rising)* Thank you...

> **PITTER** *hands her a large envelope, and opens others.*

> *She crosses to the desk, and stands near it opening the envelope; she takes out a document, looks at it, smiles, and puts it down slowly, in searching thought.* **PITTER** *looks up at her.*

> From my lawyer. The renewal of the lease of this house, which I sent for, to sign. *(Looking at the paper)* For twenty years beginning next month.

PITTER *(half-rising)* Would you like me to witness it for you?

DILYS I don't think I am going to sign it.

PITTER I thought you said...

DILYS I have changed my mind.

PITTER *(after a pause)* May I know why?

DILYS I don't exactly know why myself, yet.

PITTER Is that reasonable?

DILYS No, Mr Pitter, it is not reasonable. And I am glad. Because I know I am right.

PITTER You sound very sure.

DILYS So sure that I could weep with the certainty of it. As I once wept when a man asked me if I would join my life to his.

PITTER But not love this time?

DILYS This is beyond love. A feeling that all around you is new, and yet warm to the touch.

PITTER How long have you felt these things so deeply?

DILYS *(thoughtfully)* Last night, I was stirred. But not sure. Not yet.

PITTER When was the moment you felt conviction?

DILYS When the mother of a peasant child sat in that chair, and spoke of him as he carried a lamb through the spring fields. As she spoke, I thought of my dead husband. For twelve months, every time he had come into my mind, there was a pain, like a nerve that is raw. As she looked up into my face, I pressed on that nerve, viciously. I forced myself to visualize the one thing that every night had driven me to madness—the picture of his young body rotting in the ground. And there was no pain. I love him as I have never loved him before. But there was no pain... No, I shall not bind myself to this house. I have a feeling I shall be moving on, quite soon. It is interesting...

PITTER I would say that you are over the border into a country for which we materialists have no passport, and no desire.

DILYS Is that why you have this terror of dying?

PITTER *(wincing)* That may be.

DILYS The death you know must come to you, as surely as, when I let it go, this paper will fall into this basket? *(She is holding the lease over the wastepaper basket; she lets it go; it falls)*

PITTER *(suddenly breaking down)* I have no wish to discuss it... *(He rises and goes to the window)*

DILYS I beg your pardon.

> **AMBROSE** *enters from the hall, and comes slowly into the room. He is sunk in thought, sombre and tormented. His clothes seem not the same, they are so untidy; and his hair is no longer smooth and oiled, but flows wildly from his head. He walks down, oblivious to the others.*

Would you like some food?

AMBROSE *(after a pause, absently)* I'll wait for my midday meal.

DILYS The midday meal was five hours ago.

> **AMBROSE** *starts, looks from her to* **PITTER**, *and with a tremendous effort comes back to consciousness.*

PITTER Your letters, sir.

AMBROSE About time, too... *(Sitting in the high armchair)* Let's have them.

> **PITTER** *flicks open an envelope and reads.*

> **DILYS** *moves up and sits on the sofa.*

PITTER From your bank, sir. *(Reading)* "Last month's revenue from investments, profits of undertaking, rents et cetera—"

AMBROSE How do we stand?

PITTER Up three seventy pounds on investments, up two sixty-one on profits—up twenty-three pounds on sale of old stock—

AMBROSE Old stock... Will that be the remains of the burnt-out tent?

PITTER Exactly.

AMBROSE Good going...

PITTER It was bought by—let me see—the Wood Street Children's Hospital, for an out-house.

AMBROSE Ah... If I hadn't stepped in, Pitter, you'd have thrown all that stuff away.

DILYS The children's hospital must have needed that out-house very badly, to pay twenty-three pounds for it?

AMBROSE *(brutally)* When I was a child, no living soul lifted a finger so that I should not starve. *(A pause. He waves to* PITTER *to continue)*

PITTER The reason for the urgency would be the recent fire in a local candle factory.

DILYS Ah yes, child labour... Were there many fatalities?

PITTER Fifty children dead, and twenty-three badly burnt.

DILYS Twenty-three pounds profit, from twenty-three children. A pound a child. Good going.

AMBROSE *(stiffly, with an effort)* Go on, Pitter. Up twenty-three pounds—

DILYS *(rising and coming swiftly round to him)* Oh yes, you can count every golden sovereign in your bank...but on this one day of your life, Emrys Ellis—you cannot make all that as real as the empty air between this window and that village.

AMBROSE Go on, Pitter—

PITTER *(opening another envelope)* Details of your life insurance policy—

DILYS For you cannot count the air. The breathing watching air.

PITTER *(reading)* "In return for payments agreed, at the age of fifty you will be paid the sum of two thousand pounds, at sixty, three thousand, at seventy, four thousand."

DILYS Nine thousand pounds! To celebrate, on your seventieth birthday, you shall give a dinner-party!

AMBROSE *(sardonically)* To all the social superiors who ever looked through me in public thoroughfares.

DILYS It will be a large party.

AMBROSE I shall take the Birmingham Town Hall. After coffee, I shall rise smoking a cigar, and tell them how much money I own and what I think of them. When I have chewed the cud of my own importance—

DILYS You will leave them, and stalk down the steps into your own conveyance. Four horses.

AMBROSE Black horses. With plumes. An empty carriage, with a box. The best oak, with silver handles to match my hair. I shall lie carefully in the box, and drive through the crowded streets in solitary triumph.

The clock strikes eight. A pause. DILYS *covers her face, in aversion.* PITTER *rises abruptly and goes to the window as.*

MENNA *enters slowly from the hall. She is pale and dusty, without her cloak, her hair disarranged.*

AMBROSE *stares before him.*

MENNA I am sorry to have been so long.

DILYS *(with a start)* Menna! My dear... *(Rising, and going to her)* How is he?

MENNA Isslwyn? It wasn't the typhus fever.

AMBROSE *rises abruptly and makes to go into the dining-room, then stops to listen.*

DILYS Of course it wasn't—

MENNA It is cholera.

PITTER *(turning, aghast)* Cholera?

MENNA It must have been on one of the ships, the doctor said before he ran away. *(Wandering, in speech)* And not at all as common, he said... *(She collapses into* DILYS' *arms)*

DILYS *half carries her to the conversation-piece.*

PITTER But worse, is it not? Much worse?

DILYS This is your plague, in earnest... *(To* MENNA*)* And Isslywn?

MENNA He died about an hour ago.

PITTER *gasps.*

Could see his mattress from the window. At first I did not know who it was, he was such a dark muddy colour, and his face soaking into the pillow. They said go away, his mother is home where we sent her, with flower smells in the air, and not the smells of this place. *(Dully)* He knew me, just once, and tried to climb out, to come to me. There was blood round his mouth. He was an old man, and he is twenty, what does it mean? *(She is about to fall)*

DILYS *catches her and sits her in the conversation-piece.*

AMBROSE *hands* DILYS *a bottle of smelling-salts from the table.*

DILYS You have been standing at that window ten hours—

MENNA But when was it, when?

DILYS *(pressing the salts to her nostrils)* When was what, my darling?

MENNA That walk we had, right up to this door, when he was telling me about Balaclava and Alma, and after the war, where we were going to live...

DILYS Come to bed—

MENNA *(pushing her away, suddenly)* I must say what I have to say. His mother drove up, and I saw the doorman tell her she couldn't go in. She looked from him to me. I have only seen her pouring out tea, and smiling, as if she knew everything. But when she looked just now, I did not know her. I could tell she was thinking the same as I was...why? I know now what you meant. I have never done any harm, and I am sure he had not. I can never go to church again. He and I were making plans last night, for our children, but there is nothing wrong in plans, is there? If there is, I didn't know it. *(Bewildered, weeping)* What have we done? *(She lays back her head, exhausted. A pause)*

Far away, many voices, singing in Welsh, in solemn but rapturous harmony.

PITTER *goes to the window.*

PITTER *(excited in spite of himself)* They are all in the village street—a hundred of them!

DILYS *turns to* AMBROSE, *who sits in the desk chair, in the waning afternoon light, staring before him.*

DILYS But there has been no singing in the village since...

MENNA *(murmuring)* Wipe the blood from his mouth...

DILYS *(clasping her)* Does this take you back, Emrys Ellis? A mountain, and a child suddenly calling out for joy?

PITTER *(peering)* They are forming into single file—

MENNA *(delirious)* Where shall we be married, my love...in what church...

PITTER And moving slowly this way—

MENNA *(with a sob)* No, not in church...

AMBROSE *(with a sudden last cry of resistance)* Pitter!

PITTER Yes, sir?

AMBROSE I want some cold water thrown, and you are the one to do it. Quick! Under what heading is this to go down in your book? Quick!

PITTER I must confess, sir, that this is something I am not able to classify.

A loud knock at the front door.

DILYS *hastens to answer it.*

The singing grows softer and dies away.

AMBROSE I am frightened. More frightened than I have ever been in my life.

As **DILYS** *comes back into the room.*

Stay with me— *(In panic)* —stay with me!

DILYS *(crossing swiftly, and standing behind him)* I am here.

EVAN HOWELL *comes in from the hall, elated and quietly confident. He goes to* **DILYS**.

EVAN The day is come, Mrs Parry. And the voices are quickened in song.

DILYS But Evan, the plague is come to Blestin!

EVAN The empty years are over, achin' for the children that was drowned, and wondering, "What doth it signify?"

MENNA *(who has been looking at him, dazed)* Have you seen what I have seen? A warm young face on a pillow, freezing into death, with sunlight across it?

A pause going to her, and kneeling beside her.

EVAN I have seen what you have seen, and more. For I just walk to the door where all the other soldiers lie stricken wi' the same plague.

AMBROSE *turns and listens.*

Sunk deep in the straw, yea, twenty of them, face to the wall, like poor sick puppies that the world has clean forgot. And when they look at me, behold, I see in my mind, not a score in a room full of straw, but straw for miles and miles, and on the straw twenty score of thousands, the skin of them burnt, or wasting, or wet with blood and tears that never dry. All with their eyes on me. And I nod my head as if to say, all right, lads, all right...and I come straightaway here. *(Rising, and going to* DILYS*)* Will you call his mother?

The singing begins again, nearer the house this time.

DILYS Evan, are you not the one to do that?

EVAN You are the one she is the servant of, Mrs Parry, and she would not like to push herself forward, unseemly.

DILYS *crosses to the kitchen.*

BET *appears at the top of the stairs.*

AMBROSE *rises and retreats to the centre of the room, panic-stricken.*

BET *comes downstairs, folding up her apron. She is timid, but her eyes are shining.*

DILYS You have changed your clothes, Bet.

BET Yes, Mrs Parry, my Sunday best. I was hoping you would not mind. *(She comes down further)*

DILYS Why are you in your best?

BET With that singing, I think, well, it is the least his mother can do. I had got it ready, for deep inside of my heart I feel this coming a long time now.

EVAN *(advancing)* Where is he?

BET In my kitchen, blowing cold on to a bowl of porridge. You got to keep your strength up now, my lad, I said. And after that Welsh talkin' you just done to me, I said, your mouth will be dry.

AMBROSE Tell from the beginning of the day.

EVAN *sits in the desk chair.*

Pitter, write it down after, for us to examine close. Cold, cold and close... *(To* **BET***)* From the beginning.

MENNA *sits on the conversation-piece.*

The singing dies away; silence.

BET *(hesitatingly looking at* **DILYS***)* This morning start like any other day. I scold him— *(She sees the others looking at her, and subsides in an agony of shyness)*

DILYS *(gently)* Tell us, Bet... *(Slowly and instinctively, she sits on the stairs, at* **BET***'s feet)*

BET *stands halfway up the stairs, her hands crossed over her folded apron, with the others grouped below her,* **PITTER** *standing watching in the corner by the window. The setting sun gilds with light the figure of the mother. There hovers over the scene the spirit of a medieval painting.*

BET I scold him for leaving the chopper out all night, he keep to hisself for ten minutes like boys do, and off to market, whistling. Same as any other day.

EVAN And as he cometh home from market, he meet Lissy Post, that spoke to him that Isslwyn Soldier hath brought the plague to Blestin. *(To* **BET***)* Is it not?

BET That's right, Evan. And he come home, and before he was walking through the back door I say—hallo, something happened!

AMBROSE Wait a minute—I must know everything... How could you tell?

BET From his step? For with the step of a boy he went out; and he came back like he got a lot on his mind.

EVAN The step of a man.

BET And he came straight to me, and he say, in the Welsh, "Dry your hands, Mam," he says, "and sit at the table." I look at him, quite soft. "Sit down?" I say, "how can I sit down, middle of washin' up?" An' then he smile and say, very quiet, "I am a servant as well, Mam fach," he say, "the servant of my Father."

DILYS He said that?

BET Not boasting, you know, I bring him up not to boast. He said it like a little lad would, only he said it like it was true.

AMBROSE Had he ever said anything like that before?

BET Goodness me no, I never encourage such talk. I just bring him up to say his prayers, and tell him about God. *(Thoughtfully)* Though from the start, something tell me there was little need; for he knowed it all already. In my heart, before ever he come into the world, I knowed a lot of things about him and me; but never like to say them out loud.

PITTER You sat at the table?

BET And he begin to talk. "Mam," he say, "thank you for all you done for me," he say, "but my way is marked for me." And then he tell me about his Father, that his Father was broken-hearted to let him go, for He had lost him once before. And every time he see the rain come down, he say to me across the table, he think of his Father crying to see him go. "You see, Mam," he say, "the world is in a poor way again, for many are wicked, and them that is not wicked is weak, and there is a lot of stiff necks about," he say, "and the rest got to suffer for it, and that is not right. And my Father," he say, "to show the world that He think more of them than they do themselves, He is sending me." Then I put him to the sink, to wash his hands clean of the farm dirt, and me upstairs to get into my best. Only a boy he is, but he make it sound very nice, I can tell you.

DILYS *rises.* **BET** *makes to move.*

EVAN Bet...are you proud?

BET *(after thought)* No, Evan, but I am honoured. *(Coming downstairs)* For the rest, wait and see, I say; if the lad is a credit to me and to the work that he is called to, good enough—

AMBROSE Is that all?

BET No. *(Turning to him)* His hands in the water, he say that the sick are waiting for him, but nothing he can do, yet, nothing. He spoke—

AMBROSE I will finish for you. He spoke of me.

BET moves to him, and looks at him.

The singing starts again, outside the house.

BET He did. "Go to Emrys Ellis," he said, "the lad that was on the mountain," he said. *(Puzzled, looking from* EVAN *to* DILYS*)* What would he ha' meant by that?

AMBROSE looks up before him, wrapt and far away.

DILYS He meant that there was once a child, who looked one night into the sky...

AMBROSE raises his hands to his bosom.

...and put his hands to his breast. Because in his breast he felt something beat its wings. And he knew it was his immortal soul.

AMBROSE And now I know again. *(Putting his palms slowly together, without knowing it, in the attitude of prayer, simple, ecstatic and involuntary)* For certain...and for ever.

The click of the kitchen door.

GWYN comes in, and goes to his mother; they stand in the shaft of evening light. He is in dirty farm clothes, in his shirt sleeves.

Singing, all down the hill.

DILYS *draws his hair hurriedly out of his eyes; he holds out his hands, she scrutinizes his nails, and nods quickly.*

During this, **EVAN** *rises, goes into the hall, signs to the crowd, and stands there.* **BET** *embraces her son, suddenly, tearfully.*

He puts his arms round her, and moves to the hall, his eyes on **EVAN**. *He stands a moment in the main doorway, bathed in the evening light.*

As the crowd sees him, the singing dies abruptly.

He goes out to them in silence, as.

The lights fade, and the curtain rises immediately on.

Scene Five

Two days later; deep in the night.

The curtains are closed, and only the lamp near the desk is fully lit; the others are turned down to their lowest point, and the room is streaked with darkness, patterned by the glow from a primitive low oil stove (portable) which stands between the two armchairs and the conversation-piece; all three are drawn more closely round it. PITTER *is asleep on the sofa: on the desk, his open notebook, on the table, a tray with brandy bottle, glass, and tea-cup and saucer; on the small table, now behind the conversation-piece, another cup and saucer.*

Far away in the village, a burst of cheering. The clock strikes four. The noise of the front door.

MENNA *comes in, cloaked and hooded. She is tired, but entranced.*

In the village a louder burst of cheering. MENNA *sees* PITTER, *crosses to the window and opens the curtains; she is standing in the glow of the full moon. Far away, a woman's voice begins to chant, in Welsh; weird, religious.* MENNA *listens till the voice dies away, then closes the curtains and turns up the other lamps.* PITTER *stirs and wakes.*

PITTER Good gracious—where am I—what time is it—

MENNA I have no idea, Mr Pitter— *(Looking round at the clock)* —past four in the morning. And you are in Mrs Parry's house, because the inn is bursting with strangers. *(She sits at the stove, in the conversation-piece)*

PITTER *(rubbing his eyes)* Of course... I have not been up as late as this since the night I came into the world. What is your news?

MENNA The plague has gone from Blestin, Mr Pitter. The soldiers are cured.

PITTER I mean your own news.

MENNA Of Isslwyn? He woke up as he was being lifted into the trap. And he was dead, Mr Pitter, dead and turning cold...

PITTER *(sitting in the low armchair)* What did he say of it all?

MENNA All he remembers is a child standing over him, washing his face in cold water, and knowing that the water was holy... *(Rising)* A miracle.

PITTER Is it the same as you imagined?

MENNA *(considering, doubtfully)* Well, it was wonderful here that first evening—and even now, it keeps breaking over me like a wave...

PITTER And in between?

MENNA I begin to think.

PITTER That's a dangerous move.

MENNA Well... When we took Isslwyn away, just now, *he* passed us, carrying two buckets of water. Would you believe it, Mr Pitter, he was looking at me with mischief in his eyes?

PITTER Mischief?

MENNA Like a little brother who had caught you out with "Well, what do you say to *this*?" And I remembered, when Isslwyn was dying, and I said those dreadful things...well, this glorious faith I am filled with...

PITTER Is a token of gratitude for favours received?

MENNA That sounds horrid.

PITTER Beginning to think always ends up in sounding horrid.

MENNA You do not think that with getting Isslwyn back, I would be required to turn into a nun, or something?

PITTER *(with a straight face)* That would surely be giving with one hand and taking away with the other?

MENNA *(solemnly)* Yes, it would... Oh, I am relieved!

Loud knocks at the front door.

They look at each other, startled.

DILYS *(offstage)* Menna—let me in—

A MAN'S VOICE *(hardly distinguishable)* Mrs Parry—if you could induce the young gentleman to give us ten minutes—

PITTER Four o'clock in the morning—who—

Louder more frantic knocks.

DILYS *(offstage)* Please go away—let me in—

PITTER Goodness—what should we do—

MENNA *runs into the hall.*

THE MAN'S VOICE We would give him every courtesy, a little talk with him personally would—

MENNA *opens the front door and lets* DILYS *in.*

Miss, if you could persuade Mrs Parry—

MENNA *(offstage)* Go away.

She bangs the front door and follows DILYS *into the room.* DILYS *is pale, tired and dishevelled, but happy. She wears a cloak and hood with a working dress underneath.*

DILYS *(taking off her cloak)* I thought I'd never get here, that hill was a nightmare.

MENNA What happened?

DILYS The roadside is thick with strangers, they must have been pouring in since early morning.

PITTER What sort of strangers?

DILYS Sightseers. I had not thought of that. Singing, drinking, playing cards. Those were two men offering me fifty pounds for a talk for the *London Times*. *(Warming her hands over the stove)* And in front of the smithy there are three men and two women under gas flares, dancing and trying to take off their clothes and screaming "Praise God" over and over again. *(Sitting on the conversation-piece)* After the hospital, it was grotesque in the extreme... *(To* **MENNA***)* How was Isslwyn's mother?

MENNA At first she would not believe it, and was hysterical with joy. Then—

DILYS Then?

MENNA It sounds disrespectful, but she was bowing to the crowd almost as if—

DILYS As if to be brought back from the dead is the least a son of hers is entitled to?

MENNA *(giggling)* Yes.

DILYS And the doctor who ran away is strolling between the beds, as if he had done it all.

PITTER The Lord is scarcely returned to earth, and vanity and hypocrisy flourish at his feet, like nettles. Do you not find all this very discouraging?

DILYS It is not easy to accept, after the wonders we have seen; but how could anybody stay on such heights, and still breathe?

PITTER And Mr Ellis?

DILYS *(after a slight pause)* Mr Ellis? He promised he would be home soon. He needs sleep badly.

A knock at the kitchen door. A pause.

BET *comes in, with a cup of tea which she puts before* **DILYS**, *who murmurs "Thank you". She takes* **DILYS**'s *cloak and hangs it up in the hall.*

She is my servant. That's hard to get used to.

PITTER It embarrasses you?

DILYS It would, if I did not know how much more it would embarrass her to be treated as anything else.

BET *returns, and crosses towards the kitchen.*

Thank you, Bet.

BET *hesitates, and turns.*

BET Escuse me, Mrs Parry...is he behaving all right?

DILYS *looks up at her, then takes her hand, with a smile.*

DILYS Yes, Bet. He is behaving all right... *(Kissing her hand, gently, then gently letting it go, dreamy, tired)* When I'm away from him, I see him with a light round his head. But, in that hospital—he is a child running messages, his hair in his eyes, humble and hard-working. The crowd outside can never dirty that. He asked me specially about the crowd; the only time he spoke of himself. "Just because I have done a miracle," he said, "they will not expect it every day, will they? Because my Father is the one to say when I do a miracle and when I do not."

DILYS *drinks her tea.*

BET And I told him, in that kitchen, I said, "Your Father will not say yes to them miracles, neither, only once in a blue moon," I said. *(Collecting cups and saucers)* For if people is going to be brought back from the dead right and left, in no time the earth is going to be shocking over-crowded.

She goes back into the kitchen.

PITTER Her commonsense is like a rock.

DILYS A rock we shall cling to, time and time again.

PITTER We?

DILYS Emrys Ellis and I. *(Catching his eye, then looking at* **MENNA,** *who is nodding with sleep)* Come along, child... *(Propelling her to the stairs)* You've worked hard today, into bed and not another word.

MENNA Good-night, Auntie, thank you...

She runs upstairs and disappears.

PITTER How is Mr Ellis?

DILYS *(putting down her cup, on the table)* You asked that before, you sly old thing.

PITTER How has he been at the hospital?

DILYS More a child than the real one. When he is not working himself, he sits and follows him with his eyes: it is touching to see him. But I'm worried. That is what I meant about the heights. The climbing down is not easy.

PITTER I would hazard that you are helped by being only half Welsh. What might be heady Celtic blood is watered by a canny Saxon father?

DILYS *(smiling)* No doubt.

A knock at the front door.

(hurrying to it) He's home...

She goes into the hall and is heard opening the front door.

A WOMAN'S VOICE Does Mrs Parry live here?

DILYS *(off, puzzled)* Will you come in?

> **MRS LAKE** *enters the room. She is a handsome elegant Englishwoman of* **DILYS***'s age, dressed for travelling, in hat and cloak. To begin with, her social graces are to the fore; her manner, even in the houses of strangers, is that of an accomplished hostess. A little later, there emerges a diamond-hard core of materialism, calculating but shrewdly fair.*

PITTER *(rising, in susprise)* Mrs Lake!

MRS LAKE Good evening, Pitter; good morning, rather. Don't tell me *that* is Mrs Parry?

DILYS *comes back into the room.*

PITTER Mrs Parry, may I present Mrs Lake, of Birmingham.

MRS LAKE Oh, Pitter, make it at least an elegant suburb! *(Looking* DILYS *up and down, swiftly)* Mrs Parry, how do you do?

DILYS How do you do, Mrs Lake? *(Instinctively, her manner becomes social too)*

MRS LAKE I trust you'll forgive this most untimely call, but my coachman saw lights in the house.

PITTER When did you leave Birmingham?

MRS LAKE *(peeling off gloves)* Don't ask me; this morning, or yesterday morning, some time.

DILYS Good gracious—you must have something to eat, at once—

MRS LAKE It is more than kind of you, but my servants packed a picnic basket.

DILYS Oh. Take off your cloak, do, and sit down—

MRS LAKE Thank you... What a peculiar atmosphere in this village, Mrs Parry, worse than Hampstead Heath, and those policemen! *(Putting down her bag and cloak)* I thought my worst sins had been discovered. *(Sitting on the conversation-piece)* One of them said it's to do with a child whom somebody is passing off as the new Messiah, of all things. *(To* PITTER, *warming her hands)* If that is Ambrose's idea of a new circus attraction, he has gone too far, even for me. What is it all about?

PITTER It is not easy to explain—

DILYS *(quickly)* There was an outbreak of cholera in the military hospital here—

MRS LAKE Cholera! *(Starting)* Good gracious—

DILYS The alarm is over—a local doctor has effected a new cure. Hence the celebrations. *(She sits on the low armchair)*

MRS LAKE Ah... I have a horror of illness. Especially in the country, I do dislike the country, don't you? All these trees, each quite different. I like people, quantities of people, preferably round a table, don't you? Please don't bother to answer any of these vapid questions, I ask them purely out of nervousness.

DILYS I am nervous too.

PITTER *sits in the high armchair, to listen.*

MRS LAKE *(seeing his face, alive with curiosity)* You look exhausted, Pitter, go to bed. Curfew!

PITTER *rises, and goes sheepishly upstairs.*

DILYS *(as he goes)* You are up to his tricks, I see.

MRS LAKE I have known him for years. Nearly as long as I've known Ambrose. *(A pause. Brisk and taut, her social manner gone)* Where is Ambrose?

DILYS Still at the hospital.

MRS LAKE The hospital? He is ill?

DILYS He has been working.

MRS LAKE Working? In a hospital? Ambrose?

DILYS He should be home directly.

MRS LAKE *(sharply)* Home?

DILYS The inn is so full that he and Mr Pitter are staying with me.

MRS LAKE Yes— *(Flicking a piece of paper from her bag)* —he makes it clear that he is with you.

DILYS May I know what he wrote?

MRS LAKE *(reading)* "Something has happened which makes it impossible for me to return, something which has changed the course of my life. Care of Mrs Parry, Blestin."

DILYS *(smiling)* Not a model of tact.

MRS LAKE Mrs Parry, I am determined not to humiliate myself, but our time is short. I have known Ambrose Ellis intimately since he came as a rapscallion travelling showman and pitched his tent on a property of mine; I helped him with advice over this circus, and turned it from a joke into a respectable money-making concern. He has several times asked me to marry him, and each time I told him that when he was on the way to becoming a gentleman and the owner of twenty thousand pounds, I would consider it. With luck he may turn into both, and I shall have had a hand in his success. So I have the right to ask you not to foster this fancy he has taken to you. That is all.

DILYS It is very interesting, Mrs Lake, and—I am sure—true: except for one trifling detail. Mr Ellis has not taken a fancy to me.

MRS LAKE *(taken aback)* He has not?

DILYS And I have not taken one to him.

MRS LAKE You have not?

DILYS No.

MRS LAKE Then— *(Showing her letter)* —who is this woman he talks about?

DILYS He does not talk about any woman, he says—does he not? —that "the course of his life is changed."

MRS LAKE *(becoming exasperated)* But that is what I said! Who is this creature?

DILYS I am afraid, Mrs Lake, you are faced with something more dangerous.

MRS LAKE Rubbish, what could be more dangerous than another woman? "The course of his life is changed" – what does it mean?

DILYS I shirk the answer to that.

MRS LAKE *(sharply)* Why?

DILYS *(almost as sharply)* Because if one spent a week framing it, you would not begin to understand it.

MRS LAKE *(rising)* I have never before been accused of either stupidity or want of education.

DILYS I am accusing you of nothing. How could I blame you for lacking a quality you could never have possessed?

MRS LAKE What quality is that?

DILYS *(searching for a word)* Humanity.

MRS LAKE Humanity? *(At a loss)* I dislike Tennyson, if that's what you mean.

DILYS *(smiling)* Not entirely.

MRS LAKE I pride myself on being a woman of the world.

DILYS A woman is certainly that, who can hold a man at arm's length for ten years, until she has both mended his manners and counted his pennies... No, Mrs Lake— *(Crossing)* —I must leave you to him... *(Seeing the tray on the table, and hesitating)* I ought to suggest a glass of brandy to give you courage, but I am afraid you have no need of it.

MRS LAKE Thank you.

> **DILYS** *starts to go upstairs, then turns.*

DILYS I should like to say one thing. I know that in the past, once he had made up his mind, nothing moved him. But this is the turning point in his life; I have a feeling that he cannot *know* his mind, as yet. How can he be sure, when for so long he has stifled the true half of himself? You know the other half so well. I beg you not to take an unfair advantage.

A knock at the front door.

He's here—

She turns to go.

MRS LAKE Are you insinuating that one half of his character is to be a sealed book?

DILYS Yes.

MRS LAKE *(her temper lost)* You, who have known him three days, have the temerity to say that to me, who taught him how to use a knife and fork?

DILYS *(coldly)* I congratulate you.

> **DILYS** *goes upstairs.*

> **MRS LAKE** *stamps her foot angrily, looks round towards the hall, goes up quickly to the fireplace, and looks at herself in the mirror, as.*

> **BET** *crosses from the kitchen to the hall.*

BET *(offstage)* Mr Ellis!

She returns, opening wider the main door.

Is he all right?

AMBROSE *(offstage)* Fast asleep.

BET *(with a sigh of relief)* Oh...fast asleep, that is good...

> **AMBROSE** *enters slowly past her; he carries* **GWYN** *in his arms. He walks in a dream of serenity, across towards the stairs.*

> **MRS LAKE** *is hidden from him by the screen.*

(closing the main door) Stockings comin' down, ttt... *(Following* **AMBROSE***)* Hungry?

> **AMBROSE** *begins to go upstairs.*

AMBROSE Before we left, I made him eat. All he wants is sleep.

BET I got his bed ready –

AMBROSE *disappears;* BET *follows him.*

A pause. MRS LAKE *moves forward a step, and looks after them, puzzled and uneasy.*

AMBROSE *comes downstairs again, still in a mystic dream. He blinks in the strong light and sits in the desk chair.*

BET *comes downstairs.*

MRS LAKE *watches them.*

(on the stairs) He is sleeping the peacefullest sleep I ever did see him in... *(Going to* AMBROSE, *shy but confident)* Mr Ellis bach, will you do something for me? So many things that I have not got the words for, and with your better schoolin', you have. Tell me what you are thinking.

AMBROSE I am thinking... *(Raising his arms, and weighing them, wonderingly)* ...that I have carried him home, two miles uphill, and I can feel my arms as light as the air.

BET Which road was it you come?

AMBROSE The back way, through the fields.

BET *(sitting, impulsively, on the footstool)* Tell me a bit more.

AMBROSE *(after a pause, looking at her, speaking slowly and simply)* I am thinking that though I may never speak again of that journey until the hour before I die, it is not lost. I stopped and looked at the moon: the same face that blessed the hillside of Bethlehem. Somewhere, there was a woman singing: a holy song. I could even hear him breathing, and I looked down. In the shadow of his cheek there was the sorrow of the world. I moved on. But it was more than walking. I spanned the earth with one healing step.

BET *(after a pause, her hands folded, smiling)* No, that journey is not lost... *(Rising, crossing, and going upstairs)* You get some sleep too, no sense in gettin' too deep too quick.

She disappears.

AMBROSE *gets up, then sits again, his eyes closed, content but suddenly exhausted.* MRS LAKE *comes down and stands boldly in front of him.*

MRS LAKE Thank you for your letter.

AMBROSE *open his eyes and sees her. He stares at her long and widely.*

AMBROSE What?

MRS LAKE I said thank you for your letter.

AMBROSE *(blankly)* Yes... I'm sorry, I was not expecting to see you just then.

MRS LAKE Have you been drinking?

AMBROSE No. But I was miles away. *(Rising, recovering himself, confusedly)* I beg your pardon...but you must have been travelling for hours. And you look as fresh as if—

MRS LAKE I make it my business to look fresh, you know that. Your collar is creased. Are you not going to kiss me?

He puts his hand to his collar, mechanically, and kisses her, just as mechanically.

AMBROSE How is everything?

MRS LAKE Not entirely satisfactory. *(Sitting in the low armchair)* The circus was closed last night.

AMBROSE *(staring at her)* Closed?

MRS LAKE Lights out and tarpaulins up. *(She takes a scent-bottle from her bag and sprays her handkerchief)*

AMBROSE But I have never had it idle since I opened it!

MRS LAKE Well, you have it idle now. Bills all over the city. "Ambrose Ellis Circus Cancelled".

AMBROSE *(thoroughly roused)* But why?

MRS LAKE Workmen. The labourers in the stables—you remember, there was trouble with them last winter—

AMBROSE Ah, wages... *(Pacing, the autocrat again)* I was a fool not to leave Pitter there... What brought it to a head?

MRS LAKE It seems that the wife of one of the ostlers died, and somebody spread the rumour that she was under-nourished.

AMBROSE *stops pacing. A pause.*

AMBROSE I see.

MRS LAKE If you did not provide the employment, they would have no nourishment at all, over or under. You treat them extremely well, I think, look at that Christmas dinner you gave them, with a glass of port each and a cigar. The impertinence!

AMBROSE *(slowly)* And a paper hat for each guest, with my name on it?

MRS LAKE And a great deal was made of three children with rickets, which always sounds to me like a very dull game. *(A pause. She shuts her bag)*

AMBROSE *turns slowly and looks upstairs.*

How is the musical dwarf? You'll need him now.

AMBROSE I wish you had not come so soon. I am not ready to meet you yet. *(Crossing, and sitting opposite her, with decision, in the conversation-piece)* But I will try to tell you what has happened to me. You know about...this week, here?

MRS LAKE You mean this child?

AMBROSE He has called me to be a servant of God.

A pause. She looks at him.

MRS LAKE It is just as well I am no church-goer, or I'd find this joke in poor taste.

AMBROSE He has called me to a mission, as definitely as a servant of government is called to his.

MRS LAKE Am I expected to take seriously what you were saying to her just now?

AMBROSE Whatever I said I meant more truly than anything I ever spoke in my life.

A pause. She stares, rises, and stares again.

MRS LAKE I have known you moody and viciously discontented, but this is new. I am bewildered—

AMBROSE You will never be anything else, until you accept the fact that all the time you have known me, I have been completely untrue to myself.

MRS LAKE I see. The night you stormed at me, that if you were not financially independent by the time you were thirty-five, you would hang yourself—was that a sham? The midnight oil you have burned, straining to squeeze shillings into your money-box—am I to believe that all the time you were really at your devotions?

AMBROSE *(wincing)* Don't...

MRS LAKE Have you forgotten your rage when Harvey's Fair filched that London circuit from under your nose, and how you plotted for a whole year to pay him back—

AMBROSE *(rising, and pacing, in agitation)* It is all true, and as vile as you make it sound—

MRS LAKE Look at the way you started up just now when I gave you bad news about your business—you were Napoleon again!

AMBROSE *(with a cry)* No! *(Confused)* Was I? It was habit... Was it? *(Half to himself, desperately)* I must be honest now, at all costs, I must be honest... No, not just habit—I *was* angry, I was the little man of power again. I might never have seen *him...* *(His hands to his head, desperately)* I'm tired, am I not? Suddenly dead tired...

MRS LAKE This Mrs Parry, has she been called to a mission too?

AMBROSE She believes in it, and in me.

MRS LAKE She does, does she? *(Raising her voice)* I begin to understand—

AMBROSE *(coldly)* Now you are showing signs of the vulgarity you spent years trying to get rid of in me. *(He moves away)*

A pause.

MRS LAKE *(changing tactics)* I have not come all this way to quarrel with you, my dear. Let us look squarely at this—this evangelical bout. *(She sits in the high armchair)*

AMBROSE Very well. *(He sits in the other armchair)*

MRS LAKE What are your practical intentions?

AMBROSE Practical... *(On the defensive)* I have not thought yet—

MRS LAKE But, my dear, you must! A child asleep under the moon is touching enough, if you like that sort of picture; but there's such a thing as daylight, and it is not far off! Let us think together. You will sell the circus, of course. What will you do with your money?

AMBROSE I shall—I shall have little use for it...

MRS LAKE You will give it away. Obviously. What will you live on? Incense? Hymn-singing? Or just air?

AMBROSE I shall keep back enough for necessities—

MRS LAKE Will that include wines and cigars? If it doesn't, my dear—it will be a vile-tempered preacher who will step up into the pulpit!

AMBROSE Preacher? Pulpit?

MRS LAKE But you'll take holy orders, of course?

AMBROSE *(tormented)* Of course not—no—

MRS LAKE But how else, in a Christian country, will you carry any authority? I'll travel miles to see you in that collar. And frankly, I shan't be the only one—the Midland Race Club, to start with, in a body! So you are not going to become a clergyman?

AMBROSE I intend to make up for the self-seeking I have been guilty of, half my life. I shall use whatever talents I have for the service of my fellow-creatures.

MRS LAKE Your talents... You mean your genius for making money out of the lower classes?

AMBROSE I have others. Surely I have others...

MRS LAKE I shall be interested to hear. Name them.

AMBROSE O God... This vision you have granted to me—I can feel it sliding—melting... Oh God— *(Falling to his knees)* —do not let it go...

MRS LAKE *rises, looks at him, startled. A pause. She hides an involuntary smile. He looks at her, his mood of exaltation ebbing visibly.*

I'll speak your thought for you. It is easier to kneel with dignity than to get up again.

He laughs bitterly, and jerks to his feet.

MRS LAKE *(implacably)* So you are not going to go into the Church—

BET *runs downstairs, distressed.*

BET I beg your pardon, sir—

AMBROSE *(perturbed)* Yes?

BET He is mutterin' terrible, sir, in his sleep, as if there was something troublin' him bad—

AMBROSE Troubling him?

BET About farmyards, he say all the time, in the Welsh; nearly daylight, he say, and all the farmyards is wakin' up, and then asking for you, sir!

AMBROSE For me?

He runs wildly upstairs.

The woman is heard singing, nearer than before.

BET *(collecting herself, embarrassed)* Escuse me. *(Taking* **DILYS**'s *teacup from the table)* Would you like a cup of tea?

MRS LAKE No thank you.

BET moves towards the kitchen. She looks at MRS LAKE with sudden wide eyes, then uncertainly upstairs, round the room, and back at MRS LAKE.

The woman's voice, singing.

BET Please go.

MRS LAKE *(dumbfounded)* What did you say?

BET It is wrong, you to be here. I cannot say why, but it is wrong. *(Imploringly)* Please go.

MRS LAKE stares at her, half frightened.

AMBROSE comes back downstairs.

The woman's voice dies away.

AMBROSE Fast asleep.

BET *(with a start of relief)* Thank you, sir. *(To* **MRS LAKE,** *unsure and frightened herself)* Good-night.

She goes into the kitchen.

AMBROSE looks after her, serene and confident again.

MRS LAKE Who is that woman?

AMBROSE She is his mother.

MRS LAKE But of course! The whole business is leading up to a request for money.

AMBROSE *(going to her, strong and calm)* Listen to me. He has, this week, with his hands and with his eyes, cured a score of mortally sick men.

MRS LAKE Have you never heard of healing by faith? Of the pilgrims who travel—

AMBROSE In a house not a mile from here, there lies a solider peacefully asleep, who not many hours ago was dead.

MRS LAKE *(startled)* Dead?

AMBROSE You have nothing to say. You, who even more than Pitter, have an answer to everything...you have no answer to that.

MRS LAKE He couldn't have been dead, he was obviously in a trance, any doctor—

AMBROSE He was dead, and he was brought back to life by a miracle.

MRS LAKE Performed by a child?

AMBROSE And I have been called to show that child to the world.

A pause. She looks at him.

MRS LAKE She was right. This is a side of you I have never seen. *(She walks away, then a sudden thought comes to her. She turns to him, a new note in her voice)* You have been called to show him to the world, did you say?

AMBROSE I have.

MRS LAKE Now I begin to see where I am! *(Sitting in the conversation-piece)* Ambrose, I'll make a guess...that this boy implied that he had chosen you specially?

AMBROSE *(stepping forward)* He told his mother—

MRS LAKE Of course he did—and *she* told *you*...! Do you know, Ambrose, these people have done what nobody in the whole of commercial Birmingham has ever been able to do...they have touched you on your weakest spot!

AMBROSE *(slowly)* And what is that?

MRS LAKE Your vanity.

She sits in the low armchair, shaken.

Has that struck home, Ambrose! I thought it would! Now go on being honest. You have not worked out the future of this masquerade, but you have in your mind the broad emotional picture. And that picture is of you—didn't you say—spanning the earth with one healing step. That sounds very fine, but I thought *he* was the healer?

AMBROSE I meant that he will give me the power to lessen the sufferings of mankind—

MRS LAKE By performing the miracles yourself?

AMBROSE Of course not—I meant... *(With a groan)* I meant... *(He rises and looks entreatingly upstairs)*

MRS LAKE I'll tell you. *(She rises and walks swiftly to him)* Ambrose...

As he turns slowly and faces her.

You meant that you saw yourself as the discoverer of this unique child, striding through the contryside with one hand on this shoulder—the other cleaving a way through millions of marvelling onlookers.

AMBROSE Go on.

MRS LAKE The great pioneer, the centre of an adoring multitude... the showman. Was this new life to be so new after all? Was there not to be a fair smacking of the old circus about it?

A pause. Imperceptibly the lamps begin to dwindle.

AMBROSE *sits heavily, in the desk chair.*

AMBROSE I will be honest. And I will say you are right... *(Slowly)* A man is tied to the stake of his own limitations. I have made a fool of myself. *(In desperation)* But the eyes—on each side of the road... I said to myself then, never can I forget the worship in these silent faces—

MRS LAKE Have you seen the village now—no, you came through the fields, didn't you say? You were lucky, the place is crawling with sightseers.

AMBROSE Sightseers?

The woman is heard singing, nearer, this time. Her voice is now hoarse and tuneless.

MRS LAKE My dear man, they are all here, the old race-course crowd, playing dice under the hedges, swilling out of bottles, women and all. You heard a woman singing, didn't you, a holy song? I passed her as she sang; sprawled against the milestone, her hair caked with mud... Listen!

The woman singing: a note ends in tipsy laughter. Other voices answer.

They have been making a rare night of it, because in the morning they will insist on seeing some tricks for themselves. Will he oblige, do you think? There'll be trouble if he doesn't! Would you like to hear what they shouted after my carriage, with "Christ" every other word—

AMBROSE *(his hands to his ears)* No—no!

A pause. The woman laughs idiotically; her voice trails away.

MRS LAKE *(sitting on the stool beside him, more gently)* But, Ambrose, this is the sort of phenomenon you have been chasing for years! "What my jaded public needs," I've heard you say, "is for Joan of Arc to turn up in Birmingham."

AMBROSE *(brutally)* And Joan of Arc is small fry compared with this. Eh?

MRS LAKE That is the first thing you have said which is true to yourself—Ambrose, the relief! If you were to engage him now, your circus, in three days—

AMBROSE No, not the circus! *(Rising, and striding, desperately)* I cannot rub my nose in any of that any more, it would make me retch—

MRS LAKE You want to give up the circus?

AMBROSE I must—this has at least made me certain of that—

MRS LAKE But my dear, you can! To-morrow! *(Crossing to her bag)* The day after you left, Lord Millotson came to dinner, and what do you think he agreed, which I had been angling for since Sir John Ferries was killed at Sebastopol? To offer to Ambrose Ellis the chairmanship of the Millotson Strand Company!

A pause. AMBROSE *turns and stares at her.*

AMBROSE The chairmanship?

MRS LAKE *(searching in her bag)* When you hardly hoped for a seat on the board, you remember? *(Holding out a document)* There you are, what you have been hankering after ever since I have known you. Complete escape from the provincial treadmill, a mantle of social dignity.

AMBROSE More money, more power. *(Taking the document)* More power, more money.

MRS LAKE *(crossing to the window)* And the world must agree that you have worked extremely hard, and deserve it. *(Opening the curtains)* I hope you appreciate the trouble I have taken.

A faint grey shaft of light cuts across the room.

It's daylight... A horrible cold morning too. The village looks as dead as a cemetery. *(Shivering)* Creatures lying about like corpses, ugh... *(She puts on her cloak)*

AMBROSE *sinks onto the conversation-piece.*

I shall rest at the inn, one of the policemen is arranging it for me.

AMBROSE *half-rises, mechanically.*

Don't bother, dear, Robinson is at the gate. Come down to me for luncheon, and then we'll decide when to leave. Have a sleep, put on a starched collar, and don't get morbid. *(Starting to go, then turning, in the main doorway)* You are coming back with me?

AMBROSE Yes...

MRS LAKE What a blessing it is that I understand you.

She goes into the hall.

AMBROSE *(hardly speaking)* I am coming back...

The sound of the front door closing behind **MRS LAKE**.

The lamps flicker to almost nothing.

AMBROSE *sits in the ghastly light of dawn. He sees the document in his hand, unfolds it, and looks down at it. He hears something, lifts his head, and listens.*

Far away the crowing of a cock, three times.

The lights fade, and the curtain rises immediately on.

Scene Six

Early the following evening. The stove is in the same place, still lit.

EVAN sits on the music chair, MENNA *in the conversation-piece; both are anxiously waiting. The clock strikes eight.*

A pause. EVAN *rises and looks out of the window.*

MENNA Can you see the hospital gate?

EVAN I can see the wall that is nigh to it. Edwards Blacksmith will stand there and take the cloth from off his neck to wave it, if the doctor hath said yes, he will come to this house.

DILYS comes downstairs, wearing an apron and carrying a bowl with crumpled towels over it; she looks worn and distressed.

MENNA *(rising)* The soup is on the stove, is there anything else?

DILYS You are a good girl—any sign of the doctor?

EVAN Not yet.

DILYS puts her hand to her head with a gesture of desperation.

MENNA Is there nothing more we can do without him?

DILYS I even know the locker where he keeps the drugs, but I would not dare try to mix them. *(Controlling herself)* We must be patient. *(She is suddenly overcome with tiredness, and sinks into the desk chair)*

EVAN *(after a pause)* Hoping no wrong in asking, Mrs Parry, but...when Mr Ellis leave, was he in a bad way with himself?

DILYS I have no idea what state of mind he was in, Evan, he left before any of us was up.

MENNA Where has he gone to?

DILYS Birmingham, I expect.

MENNA *(looking at* EVAN*)* Birmingham?

DILYS It is where he came from.

MENNA *(after a pause)* How is...how are the symptoms?

DILYS Worse.

MENNA Oh no...

EVAN Any more sign of—

DILYS The cholera? There is the violent cramp, and the breaking under the skin—

MENNA No—not that—

EVAN Thirsty, is he?

DILYS Dreadfully.

MENNA Is he in great pain?

DILYS He keeps moaning and crying, and has dug his hands deep into the mattress. He keeps asking for his Father.

On the point of breaking down, she rises and hurries into the kitchen.

EVAN She was like unto a sword of hope. Is *she* losing faith?

MENNA Don't say it...

As he looks out again.

Any trace of the sightseers?

EVAN In the village road, three broken bottles. The last is gone. *(Sitting)* Ignorant tribe they was, but meaning no harm.

MENNA But were you not shocked by their attitude?

EVAN No fault of theirs, isn't it? For there is an empty part of them, in their breast, that is there to be filled. They are only waitin' to be told... One of them come and quoth to me, would I favour a picture of me in a newspaper.

MENNA The impertinence! What did you say?

EVAN I said yea.

MENNA What would you do with it?

EVAN Lay it I would in my Bible so everybody see it when I sheweth to them a passage. *(With a sigh)* Nobody will want to make my picture now.

MENNA And will you be opening your Bible as much as you have done?

EVAN *(looking at her, soberly)* I do not know, Miss Parry. I, now, I am waiting to be told.

MENNA Isslwyn said that, in another way.

EVAN Isslwyn Soldier hath taken this news to heart?

MENNA He wept, bitterly: I hardly knew him. "Why should I be alive and well," he said, "why?" And then he said, "Menna, if I could be guided now, I would turn my back on bloodshed and serve the Lord." And Evan, I would go with Isslwyn, joyfully. But how can we be sure?

EVAN How indeed? *(Rising)* With him up there, catching the plague, which in five score years none of us would deem he would do... If anything come to pass—

MENNA We must not even think it...

EVANS *turns and looks out again. He starts.*

EVAN There he is— *(Calling)* —Mrs Parry—

MENNA *(rising)* Is it the blacksmith—is he waving?

EVAN No.

As DILYS *runs in from the kitchen.*

EVAN *shakes his head.*

DILYS Oh.

EVAN And he walketh slow towards his smithy.

MENNA Which means that our last hope is gone.

DILYS The doctor refuses to leave the patients that are cured, to save the patient that cured them for him.

A pause. Outside the house, singing: hushed, beseeching voices.

They listen.

EVAN *(losing control)* Mrs Parry!

DILYS Yes, Evan?

EVAN You are strong. Stronger than Emrys Ellis. Help us!

DILYS I thought I was stronger. *(After thought)* While he struggled and shied, my faith welled up inside me; a marvellous and easy slipping away from pain. But I forgot one thing. Menna fach, I ask your pardon.

MENNA What for?

DILYS When you talked of Isslwyn, I smiled at your young devotion. I forgot that I am a woman too. I have said that I loved my husband as I can never love again, and that is true...but whatever any of us may say, whether a woman breathes with her body or with her spirit, it is only through a man that she breathes to the full.

The main door opens, and AMBROSE *enters. He is deathly tired and travel-stained, but looks curiously composed. He wears a travelling overcoat.*

EVAN *and* MENNA *see him,* DILYS *does not.*

If the faith I have nursed in Emrys Ellis...has died, then my light is put out as well.

AMBROSE *(coming down)* The doctor will be here in ten minutes.

DILYS *turns slowly and looks at him. For a moment, from now on, they look at each other steadfastly.*

MENNA But he has just refused to leave the hospital.

AMBROSE Not that one, I went straight to him this morning when I left this house, and I knew then *he* would be no good to us.

MENNA *(overjoyed)* You found another?

AMBROSE The best in Shropshire, they said. To save time, he has driven straight on down to the hospital, to mix the essential drugs.

DILYS *(rising)* They are in the corner ward, in a locker. The key—

AMBROSE I had remembered, and told him.

DILYS He will not miss the gate, on the way back?

MENNA I'll stand in the road, and watch out for him—

She runs into the hall and out of the front door.

AMBROSE His mother is with him?

DILYS Yes. We must be patient, and wait.

EVAN He will live?

DILYS He will live. Every drop of my blood is crying out with the thought that he will live.

The voices falter, and stop.

AMBROSE Will she tell them there is hope?

EVAN But not in the Welsh! *(Joyfully)* They will find double the comfort in the Welsh—

EVAN hurries into the hall and out of the front door.

DILYS and AMBROSE are alone. They stand, still looking at each other.

AMBROSE When I came in then, you were on the edge of despair.

DILYS But as soon as I saw your eyes, I knew that all will be well.

AMBROSE You are tired.

DILYS I am beyond tiredness. So are you.

AMBROSE Far beyond.

She hold her hands to her eyes, in deepest relief, and moves down.

DILYS Was it a dreadful journey?

AMBROSE Very long, but I was glad of it. *(Moving to her)* You see, as soon as I had...denied him... I knew that he would suffer human agony. And I had to look into the darkest corners of myself.

DILYS *(eagerly)* Tell me— *(Sitting)* —what did you find?

AMBROSE It is early to know for sure. But I think I found the truth. *(Sitting opposite her, and speaking with great certainty and calm)* Last night, I met with a shocking defeat. But I know that from that defeat, he means us to grow.

DILYS Slow and sure, we shall grow.

AMBROSE I had been seeing our future as the glorification of him personally; and when she called me the exploiter of the New Messiah, it struck home, fatally—his mother said the true thing, of course, I was getting too deep, too quickly. If I weren't, I'd have realized that his plans for our future must be very different. This week, to you and to me, he has given a new life: but it will be for us to live that life, not for him to live it for us. He, I am sure, will see fit to stay behind.

DILYS With his mother, as humble as she has always wished them to be—

AMBROSE And he will choose to send us out, to work in his name.

DILYS What sort of work?

AMBROSE *She* taunted me with being a successful man of business—that was her second weapon. But commonsense should have told me that when I did face my new life in the daylight, that would be just the time for my business talents. *(Taking a crumpled sheaf of papers from a pocket)* They are in use already.

DILYS What is all that?

AMBROSE Scribblings on the journey. Estimate for sale of circus, stocks and shares—right down to recruiting of workers, and even mileages.

DILYS For our travels?

AMBROSE Up Wales, and down Wales—we stopped for food, the doctor and I. For the first time in twenty years, I spoke my own tongue. It came back to me!

DILYS In a month you will be talking as if you had never left it.

AMBROSE For now, we shall teach in the open air—

DILYS Teach?

AMBROSE Reading and writing, to start with, then I'll try to go deeper—I wasn't a bad schoolmaster, when I wasn't smarting with insults! To make fun of me, she dressed me up as a conventional parson—but all my hope and all my strength must be in the *un*-conventional. I shall teach, as simply and truly as I can, and as you can help me to. Some will welcome us, but there will be the others—

DILYS The scoffers, and the ones with the devil in them—

AMBROSE And worst of all, the lazy ones.

EVAN *comes in from the hall, and listens to him.*

We shall find ourselves on street corners in the rain, gaped at, taunted like gipsies—

DILYS One day we shall look back, and all that will be nothing.

AMBROSE In those villages, I looked into their faces. Empty inquiring eyes... They were my eyes, all of them.

DILYS Staring deep into you out of your own thwarted childhood...

EVAN A great multitude, waiting to be told...

DILYS Waiting to hear again, fresh and new, the story of the
   Son of God.

EVAN Waiting to be assured that they are not beasts of the field—

DILYS And that their salvation is in their own hands.

   MENNA *runs in from the hall.*

MENNA The doctor is walking up the drive!

AMBROSE *(eagerly)* I'll take his box—

   He hurries into the hall and out of the front door.

   MENNA *looks at* **DILYS**, *smiling.* **DILYS** *gives a sigh of
   contentment, presses* **EVAN**'s *arm and moves towards the
   hall. She stops suddenly.* **MENNA** *moves round;* **EVAN**
   lifts his head.

MENNA What was it?

DILYS Did you feel something?

EVAN A wind. A wind of music.

DILYS Music that swept through the room—

   PITTER *hastens in from the dining-room, quill pen in
   hand.*

PITTER What was that—did you feel a wind through the house?

DILYS But the curtains should have moved—

MENNA And yet they didn't—

PITTER *(puzzled)* And I was thinking how heavy the air was
   today...

   DILYS *rouses herself, and makes a step towards the hall.
   She hears a sound upstairs, and starts back.*

   BET *comes downstairs she is pale, but very composed.*

BET *(seeing them)* Escuse me... *(She walks down another step
   or two)*

DILYS There was a wind blew through the house.

BET *stops and turns to her, simply.*

BET Yes, quite right. Just when he died. From the plague he died.

A pause. DILYS *moves towards her.*

Better not to come near, Mrs Parry fach, for this plague is a terrible thing, and I just cross his hands over his chest. I am glad to see him at rest, for I never wish to see a dog under some carriage wheels to be in such pain as that lad was. Though I shall never be the same, o' course, with him bein' my only one... Please can I thank you, Mrs Parry, for all you done. He could not ha' been treated better if he was a king.

DILYS He is more than a king.

BET Not in his own sight, Mrs Parry, escuse me, nor yet in mine. He live like any boy, and like any boy he die, too. Like them soldiers he die, his poor flesh smellin' awful wi' the plague; but no mother is bothered by that, o' course... And his face is all right. As easy as a flower. Young he was, but good company. I will go for some more warm water.

As she moves down towards the kitchen door AMBROSE *comes in slowly from the hall. He looks at* DILYS, *she looks at him.*

(turning to him) Could I speak to you, sir, for a minute?

AMBROSE There was a wind blew down the hill, and through the village. And then...

DILYS And then?

AMBROSE It rose up, into the loving sky.

He comes down, and faces BET.

BET *(to him)* He was cryin' to hisself wi' the pain, and all of a sudden, stop. And he turn to me, as if nothing the matter in the world, and speak very clear and slow. "Mam," he say in the Welsh, "go to Emrys Ellis, and say to him, that now he has looked in his heart, deep an' long, what he see there, he got to mark very careful. For I am dying," he say, "before my time, and Emrys Ellis is goin' to make his life according." And then in his pain he turn over, and never said no more than that on earth. If he had lived, and learn his letters, he would have been a lovely speaker. *(She turns to go, then stops: she is looking through the open doorway)* Diar annwyl, it is in my kitchen I will miss him.

She puts her apron to her eyes and goes into the kitchen.

Outside the watching villagers sing again.

EVAN *stumbles to the hall and looks out.*

AMBROSE *(his eyes upstairs)* The five days' wonder of Blestin is over.

DILYS And the corpse of a Welsh peasant boy waits for a grave without a name.

EVAN *(coming down)* The village hath asked for you, Emrys Ellis. All round the gate they are gathered.

AMBROSE *looks at* **DILYS**.

MENNA *goes up into the hall, to look out.*

DILYS Your work is going to start.

AMBROSE *crosses to go to the hall, then turns to* **DILYS**, *suddenly unsure.*

AMBROSE What shall I say?

DILYS Evan, how does the Lord's Prayer begin, in Welsh?

EVAN *(to* **AMBROSE***)* The Lord will help you, sir. Speak with Him homely, for He knoweth you well. Ein Tad yr hwn wyt yn y nefoedd...

AMBROSE Ein Tad— *(Faltering)* —yr hwn wyt yn y nefoedd.

EVAN Sancteiddier dy enw, deled dy deyrnas.

AMBROSE Sancteiddier dy enw— *(Turning and walking up to the hall, with more confidence)* —deled dy deyrnas...

EVAN Gwneler dy ewllys.

> **AMBROSE** *goes out through the front door, speaking under his breath.*

AMBROSE *(offstage)* Gwneler dy ewyllys...

> **EVAN** *follows him, together with* **MENNA**.

EVAN *(offstage)* Megis yn y nef—

AMBROSE *(offstage)* Megis yn y nef—

EVAN *(offstage)* Felly ar y ddaear hefyd—

AMBROSE *(offstage)* Felly ar y ddaear hefyd—

> *During this,* **DILYS** *takes off her apron, watching* **PITTER** *as he goes down to the desk and takes up his notebook.*

DILYS What will you do?

PITTER I have saved enough to retire. I shall finish my book.

DILYS Why?

PITTER This week in Blestin I have seen strange things. I have seen faces that had been as heavy as clay, turn into shining lamps.

DILYS Yesterday, you said it had made you wonder. What of today?

PITTER All the facts are capable of rational explanation. Before the birth, hallucination on the part of the mother. The music heard by the village; self suggestion induced by years of suppressed emotionalism. The miracle at the hospital: catalepsy. The child's fore-knowledge of Mr Ellis's arrival...

fortune-telling. Mmm... *(Looking upstairs)* ...I should hazard that he is *not* the Messiah.

DILYS *(softly)* But we believe that he is.

PITTER *(turning and looking at her)* If you believe, then he is. *(Taking out his watch, and winding it, thoughtfully)* And whatever sand we may wager your faith is built on, the work you will do will be good. I, and those like me, may be in every way better informed, but we have nothing like that. Have we even any more than the mole, piteous in his deformity, burrowing blindly through the dank earth, when an inch above his snout there is air, and sun, and the wild stinging cleansing rain...are we better than the mole? *(He stands thoughtful a moment, then snaps his watch to)*

BET *enters from the kitchen carrying the bowl full of clean water, her apron over it. She starts to go upstairs.*

The voices of the mourners outside are lifted again.

BET *stops and listens. But the singers are no longer mournful; the voices throb with joyful confidence, the same hymn of hope as when they first sang.*

DILYS *stands where she is, her apron folded over her hands, her eyes calmly before her.*

In the waning light, the mother turns and looks at PITTER. *She stands a moment, compassionate, transcended. His eyes quail before hers, and his head is slowly bowed. The voices swell, as she turns and walks up to the room where lies the body of the dead child.*

The curtain falls.

Lightning Source UK Ltd.
Milton Keynes UK
UKHW021133301119
354479UK00010B/727/P

9 780573 016530